A MAN
LIKE NO
OTHER

A MAN LIKE NO OTHER

R. Earl Allen

The Popular Elective Series brings you
affordable books written by quality authors
and planned especially for group study. An
expertly prepared leader's guide is available
with each book.

VICTOR

BOOKS a division of SP Publications, Inc.
WHEATON, ILLINOIS 60187

Offices also in
Whitby, Ontario, Canada
Amersham-on-the-Hill, Bucks, England

Recommended Dewey Decimal Classification: 232
Suggested Subject Heading: JESUS CHRIST

Library of Congress Catalog Card Number: 84-50142
ISBN: 0-89693-374-1

VICTOR BOOKS
A division of SP Publications, Inc.
           Wheaton, Illinois 60187

Contents

Dedicated
to
our children,
James Todd and Dee Allen
Steven and Joy Newcom
and
our grandchildren,
Justin Allen Newcom
Joshua Gordon Newcom
James Clinton Allen
Christina Marie Allen

1 His Wonderful Portrait

Isaiah 9:6

By inspiration, Isaiah prophetically painted a portrait of the coming Messiah which has resounded through the ages. The inspired seer broke into exalted music: "For unto us a child is born, unto us a son is given: and the government shall be upon His shoulder: and His name shall be called Wonderful, Counselor, The mighty God, The everlasting Father, The Prince of Peace" (Isa. 9:6).

The Roman world into which this Redeemer-Prince came was laden with darkness and violence. Our world also is a stronghold of darkness. In this thermonuclear era, evil has intensified. The depravity of mankind has merely become more sophisticated. "The lamps are going out all over Europe," observed a British statesman in 1914, on the eve of World War I, "and we shall not see them again in our lifetime." Now, though we have fought back the darkness and turned on a few flickering lights, the darkness does not dissipate, but only seems to pervade other areas and soon deepens.

I dogmatically declare—our only hope for light in

the darkness is Jesus Christ, the Light of the World.

The darkness of sin entered the world when Adam and Eve disobeyed God. They were exiled from the Garden of Eden, and the gate was barred by flashing swords of holiness, but God lit a candle for them with the promise of a Redeemer: Eve's seed would bruise the serpent's head (Gen. 3:15).

Down the halls of history and the corridors of the centuries reverberate the promises of God concerning Jesus Christ, the "Shiloh" of Genesis, "the coming One." God spoke "in time past unto the fathers by the prophets" (Heb. 1:1).

Moses foresaw that the Messiah would be of the descendants of Judah (Gen. 49:10). The prophet Micah pinpointed the place: "But thou, Bethlehem . . . out of thee shall He come forth" (Micah 5:2). Daniel foretold the time of His birth (Dan. 9:25-26). Malachi described the forerunner of the Messiah (Mal. 3:1). Jonah pictured in his harrowing experiences the Lord's death and resurrection hundreds of years before the Child was born in Bethlehem.

Isaiah's Masterpiece

In the hearts of humanity, the desire to know what Jesus looked like still persists. But no artist, paint as he might, has ever achieved a completely satisfying portrait of Him. How could he? How can an artist paint God with a human face?

The Gospel writers gave eyewitness accounts of His life and work. But Isaiah, who lived 700 years before His coming, portrayed with words the fullness of deity and humanity in the person of the Lord Jesus Christ.

Because Isaiah revealed so much about what Jesus is like, his book is sometimes called the "fifth Gospel," or "the Gospel according to Isaiah." Turning his heart and mind heavenward, he proclaimed, "The people that walked in darkness have seen a great light" (Isa. 9:2).

"Isaiah didn't really prophesy," Oswald Chambers wrote, "he was proclaiming—he was writing history aforetime." This prewritten history, according to God, described the eternal Son of God. "Therefore the Lord Himself shall give you a sign; behold, a virgin shall conceive, and bear a son, and shall call His name Immanuel" (Isa. 7:14).

The word *Immanuel* means "God with us." That God descended to earth in the person of His Son is the pivotal message of Christianity.

No gift more priceless, no present more precious could come to your home. No bounty more valuable could be laid at the door of the poor. No remembrance to the brokenhearted could be more comforting. No gift presented to any soul could match the indispensable fact that God came down to dwell among us.

Christ Jesus existed before the world He helped create. He lived before His incarnation in Bethlehem. He was active in the affairs of men long before Isaiah described Him. "Before Abraham was, I am," Jesus declared (John 8:58).

In the Cornwall district of England, a newcomer to one of the villages observed that it was an unusual place. He asked, "What makes this village so different?"

"John Wesley preached here a hundred years ago," he was told. "This village has never been the same since." Jesus came to Bethlehem nearly 2,000 years ago and this world has never been the same since.

Charles Lamb, the essayist, wrote: "If Shakespeare were to enter the room, I would stand in respect to him, but if Jesus Christ came into this room I would kneel in adoration."

When Napoleon ruled, the world of his day was shaken. In exile, he was guarded by 3,000 soldiers. His enemies knew he still had a strong underground force, so they assigned a small army to prevent him from regaining power. But all the legions of Rome were not able to keep Jesus Christ in the grave. All the devils in hell were unable to separate Him from the work He came to do for us.

When God sent His own Son, wrapped Him in swaddling clothes, and laid Him in the flesh-and-blood arms of a woman, God was identifying Himself with us. Immanuel—God with us! Nothing shall ever snatch Him away from us. Even death on the cross could keep Him for only three days. Then Jesus shed the grave clothes and walked out of the tomb. The grave could not imprison Him. Nothing could separate Him from the people He came to live among and die for.

Before Jesus went to the Cross, He explained to His doubtful disciples, "It is expedient for you that I go away. . . . I will send Him [the Comforter, the Holy Spirit] unto you, and when He is come, He will reprove the world of sin. . . . He will guide you into all truth" (John 16:7-8, 13).

His concern for us is never-ending! It did not begin at Calvary or at Bethlehem. It was in eternity before the foundation of the world. "Unto us a child is born; unto us a son is given"—He is ours!

A Wondrous Saviour

Isaiah pictured the Messiah's wonderful wisdom: "The government shall be upon His shoulder: and His name shall be called Wonderful, Counselor" (Isa. 9:6).

In the Bible, 256 titles are used for Jesus, attempting to describe His majesty, His deity, His humanity—all the wonder of His abilities and attributes. Yet they are altogether inadequate. Isaiah could well have put a period after the word *Wonderful*: "He shall be called Wonderful."

Wonderful! What more can we say? Perhaps the only time the word *wonderful* is used with complete accuracy is to describe Him. Well could the hymn writer exclaim, "I stand amazed in the presence of Jesus the Nazarene!"

Historians have listed "seven wonders" of the ancient world. But there are more than seven wonders about Jesus. He was wonderful in His birth; wonderful in His life; wonderful in His teaching; wonderful in His death; wonderful in His resurrection; wonderful in His ascension.

He is wonderful in His present intercession; He will be wonderful in His future return. He is *altogether* wonderful!

Some of the most highly respected Hebrew scholars claim that a comma does not belong after "Wonderful," that Isaiah declared the coming Messiah a "Wonderful Counselor." This adds to the symmetry of the passage, because all the other titles are double: mighty God, everlasting Father, Prince of Peace. In Isaiah 28:29, Isaiah described Him as "the Lord of hosts . . . wonderful in counsel, and excellent in working."

The All-Wise Counselor

Earthly counselors come in many kinds. Often they have to reply, if they are honest, "I don't know." But Jesus' counsel is always perfect: "I am . . . the truth," He declared (John 14:6). He has all the answers. Even soldiers that His enemies sent to capture Him reported in awe: "Never man spoke like this man" (John

7:46).

Solomon was reputed to be the wisest man who ever lived. Yet Jesus claimed of Himself, "Behold, a greater man than Solomon is here" (Matt. 12:42).

What is a counselor? He is a reconciler of enemies, a solver of conflicts, a moderator of differences. The Apostle Paul testified of Jesus "that God was in Christ, reconciling the world unto Himself" (2 Cor. 5:19). Jesus, the perfect Counselor, sat in the chambers of God as equal—in the beginning, before the world was formed. He helped design both its creation and its redemption.

Astute counselors need to be completely wise and just, to possess all knowledge. But earthly counselors cannot; they do not. Jesus does. Entirely righteous and sinless, He possesses undeviating rectitude. His unlimited influence with the Father enabled Him to promise, "If ye shall ask any thing in My name, I will do it" (John 14:14). He had profound influence on those with whom He dealt—which was necessary, for you can't help a person who doesn't respect you.

So wonderful was Jesus' knowledge that when He was only twelve, teachers of the Law recessed their temple classes so they could hear His wise observations. The wise men of the synagogue shook their heads; they could not account for the youth's wisdom nor did they understand His mission.

So wonderful were His teachings that large crowds hung on every word He spoke. They followed Him into the wilderness without thought of food; they didn't even carry a sack lunch. So enthralling were His words that they refused to leave; they wanted Him to keep talking. The Bread of Life that He provided deeply satisfied them. This was what they had been waiting for, what they had been hungering for.

Most of the rabbis had never preached to a crowd like that in all their years, T. DeWitt Talmadge suggested. They wagged their heads and criticized. "This foolish young man has nothing to say. He uses unorthodox methods merely to gain an audience."

Wonderful were the words of Jesus because He spoke with simplicity. The common people could understand Him. He talked to them in the language of the street—though not the language of the gutter.

Jesus spoke of the everyday aspects of life. He began one message, "If a grain of wheat fall into the ground and die..." (John 12:24). Another time He started out with, "A farmer went forth to sow..." (Matt. 13:3). Jesus took familiar things as illustrations and applied them to teach titanic truths.

His words comforted the brokenhearted. For those who were sick, He offered balm in Gilead; for those who died, resurrection. For those who sorrowed, He sympathized and urged, "Be of good cheer" (John 16:33).

This great Counselor held out His arms and said, "Come unto Me, all ye that labor and are heavy laden, and I will give you rest" (Matt. 11:28). Peter advised, "Cast all your care upon Him, for He cares for you" (1 Peter 5:7). A long time before psychiatrists of our day bought couches, the Great Physician provided an altar for the peace of the human soul.

The Peaceful Prince

Isaiah called Jesus "The Prince of Peace." Some men have assumed the title of "prince" by legend, by family ties, or by geographical boundaries. But Jesus was named Prince of Peace by divine right and function, as the author and distributor of peace. "Peace I leave with you; My peace I give unto you," He said (John 14:27). Isaiah prophesied that "the government shall be upon His shoulder," for He is the only One truly competent to rule.

Rulership is a heavy load to carry. In England, when Oliver Cromwell died, his brother assumed the right of an heir and set himself up as "protector of England." But soon thereafter, Cromwell's brother laid down that responsibility and returned to his farm. Government is a weighty burden to a man with a conscience.

But not to Jesus. He is completely adequate for the task of ruling the whole earth: "Of the increase of His government and peace there shall be no end" (Isa. 9:7). He shall be King of kings, undisputed ruler, the Prince of Peace to all men. "He shall not fail nor be discouraged, till He have set judgment in the earth" (Isa. 42:4). He will establish peace and justice for all.

Jesus is the author of peace and the only one capable of bestowing peace. To those who bow willingly to Him, giving Him the right to rule because of what He has done for us, Jesus presents perfect peace. Then we must stand with Isaiah and cry out, "He *is* a Wonderful Counselor! He *is* the Prince of Peace!" Already He is ruler in the hearts of men of every age and every race who love Him.

When Billy Graham was ministering to the United Nations troops in Korea, on a Christmas Eve he and a chaplain found a young man dying on "Heartbreak Ridge." The chaplain and Mr. Graham climbed up the slope and stooped over the soldier. The chaplain asked softly, "May I help you, son?"

"No, it's all right," the young man answered.

The chaplain marveled at the soldier's tranquility in such an hour—until, glancing down, he noticed a New Testament clutched in the soldier's hand. A finger was inserted in the page where it is recorded that Jesus said, "My peace I give unto you" (John

14:27). They knew then the basis of the dying soldier's confidence.

Jesus was born into a nation that felt itself dying. Many of God's chosen people in that day had almost given up. Four hundred years had passed since God had sent them a prophet, and it seemed that God's promises would never be fulfilled.

After Israel's height of power under David and Solomon, the nation had broken apart—ten tribes in one kingdom and two in the other. One after the other, the two kingdoms were taken into captivity and for centuries chafed under hateful oppression from foreign rulers. But Isaiah said that "the people who sat in darkness have seen a great light." The light came gradually, beginning with a young mother, a bright star, and the music of angel voices. When you have been in darkness a long while, you can't stand much light at a time.

They could scarcely believe that their Messiah had come, their Redeemer, their Counselor. "Peace on earth, good will to men!" the angels announced. The governments of earth may fail, but never the rule of the Prince of Peace. Greece might fall and Rome lose its glory, but the kingdom of God shall prevail forever.

A Portrait Etched in Blood

Isaiah's portrait of Christ features pronounced contrasts. This glorious King is also a suffering Saviour. Over the cradle in Bethlehem fell the shadow of a cross. The red ribbon of blood began in the Garden of Eden from slain animals that provided the first coat of skins for God's sinning people, Adam and Eve. It blossomed crimson from the Cross, wrapped around God's gift to us—the gift of salvation that only God could provide. And it is a personal gift: "Unto *us* a child is born; unto *us* a son is given."

Jesus' sacrifice of suffering climaxed on the cross; it did not begin there. His family lived in poverty; the circumstances of the birth of Mary's first son evidenced their lowly estate.

His parentage was questioned; Mary suffered gossip and scorn. When Jesus taught in His hometown, He was a "prophet without honor." When He performed miracles, the townspeople asked cynically, "Isn't this the carpenter's son?" Down in Judea, the Jews inquired, "Can any good thing come out of Nazareth?"

The turbulent sea appears calm compared to the sorrow that shook His soul. While Jesus walked this earth, He was despised and rejected. He was "wounded in the house of . . . [His] friends" (Zech. 13:6). He has "trodden the winepress alone" (Isa. 63:3). He was bruised, spat on, and humiliated.

More than we can imagine, Jesus suffered. The sun burned Him; the cold chilled Him; rain pelted against His face. Thirst parched His throat; hunger exhausted Him. The cross killed Him.

But God raised Him up! For nothing "shall be able to separate us from the love of God, which is in Christ Jesus our Lord" (Rom. 8:39).

If you want to know what Jesus looked like, you may find a picture in a store or museum that partially satisfies you. But only in Isaiah can you find the perfect portrait, that divine photograph the prophet glimpsed when the mysterious shutter of God clicked seven centuries before Christ was born.

Isaiah gave us a perfect portrait of Jesus: He is *wonderful*!

There is never a day so dreary,
There is never a night so long,
But the soul that is trusting Jesus

Will somewhere find a song.
Wonderful, wonderful Jesus,
In the heart He implanteth a song:
A song of deliv'rance, of courage, of strength;
In the heart He implanteth a song.
                                        —Anna B. Russell

2 His Virgin Mother

Luke 1:35

Isaiah the prophet declared, "Behold, a virgin shall conceive, and bear a son, and shall call His name Immanuel" (Isa. 7:14). Through centuries of waiting, this sign promised by God thrilled the heart of every Jewish girl.

In Luke 1:26-27 is the beautiful account of this prophecy's fulfillment: "In the sixth month the Angel Gabriel was sent from God unto a city of Galilee, named Nazareth, to a virgin espoused to a man whose name was Joseph, of the house of David; and the virgin's name was Mary."

What kind of girl was this whom God picked to be the mother of His Son? What kind of home did she come from? What kind of childhood did she have?

The New Testament does not answer these questions for us, but God knew; "for man looks on the outward appearance, but the Lord looks on the heart" (1 Sam. 16:7). In the heart of this young girl named Mary, God found exactly what He wanted: blameless character, humility, and faith. She is not referred to as beautiful. Evidently her qualities of mind and heart were more important than mere physical attractiveness.

Mary's choice was an act of election on the part of the Lord. Mary was "highly favored" because, of all the women in the world, she was to be closest to the Son of God, especially during His early life in the home at Nazareth.

Some commentators have speculated that Mary was an orphan, because her mother and father are never mentioned, except that her father's name was probably Heli, according to Luke's genealogy. If she were an orphan, a young girl thirteen to sixteen years old would probably have been a household servant for her "board and keep."

Any serious student of church history realizes that through the centuries sharp controversies have arisen over Mary's position. About the third and fourth centuries A.D., worship of Mary began to appear, followed by the legend that Mary also was of virgin conception and birth to make her fit to bear the Holy Child.

Those who disagreed with that position tended to ignore Mary entirely. "Mary, the mother of Jesus, has not had fair treatment from either Catholics or Protestants," wrote the late Dr. A.T. Robertson, well-known Greek scholar and theologian among Southern Baptists.

This makes us stop and ask, "What is Mary's rightful place? What does the Bible say?" According to the New Testament, it is not necessary to go through Mary or anyone else to reach the heart of Jesus. "For there is one God, and one Mediator between God and men, the Man Christ Jesus" (1 Tim. 2:5).

We should neither deify Mary nor detract from her genuine importance; she deserves honor and praise, but no more. When the Child was born, the shepherds came to the stable and worshiped Him. We ought also to worship Him, not His mother.

"What think ye of Christ?" Jesus asked the Pharisees (Matt. 22:42). This is the basic question of the New Testament, not "What think ye of Mary?" The Gospels and epistles emphasize the Saviour Himself—no other.

Yet His mother, Mary, should be honored because her life fulfilled the promises of God and she accepted her position with devout faith. In Galatians 4:4, Paul declared, "God sent forth His Son, made of a woman." To be the channel of the miraculous birth of God's Son—this was Mary's chief glory.

The Angelic Promise

The Angel Gabriel appeared to Mary and assured her that "The Holy Ghost shall come upon thee, and the power of the Highest shall overshadow thee: therefore also that holy thing which shall be born of thee shall be called the Son of God" (Luke 1:35).

A person has a right to question the fact that Jesus was the only child ever born of a virgin mother, but to deny it raises even more questions. Either we accept the purity and virginity of Mary, or we are faced with unpleasant alternatives: that Jesus was Joseph's child by a premarital relationship—which Joseph definitely refuted, according to Matthew 1:19—or an illegitimate child by someone else. One theologian years ago indicated blasphemously that Jesus could have been the son of a harlot and a blond Roman soldier!

Questions raised by the Virgin Birth can be answered only on the basis of God's Word; and the fact that Jesus was virgin-born is definitely taught in the Scriptures, beginning in Genesis 3:15. The first promise of God, given in Eden, was that "the seed of the woman" would bruise the serpent's head.

Some try to minimize the problem of Jesus' birth by stating it makes little difference. Jesus could have become the Son of God at a later date, they claim. Don't you believe it! The Bible is either the Word of God, divinely inspired, or it is not. If it is divinely inspired, we must believe Matthew, Mark, Luke, and John, who assert along with Isaiah and other prophets that Jesus was born of a virgin mother.

Matthew affirmed positively that Jesus was virgin-born: "Before they [Mary and Joseph] came together, she was found with child of the Holy Ghost" (1:18). Luke described the Virgin Birth from Mary's viewpoint, giving details of the Annunciation and her pregnancy.

Mark's Gospel did not begin with the birth of Jesus. It opened with the public ministry, but his first words declare, "The beginning of the Gospel of Jesus Christ, the Son of God" (Mark 1:1). John also emphasized the Lord's heavenly origin: "In the beginning was the Word, and the Word was with God, and the Word was God. . . . And the Word was made flesh, and dwelt among us" (John 1:1, 14).

Two genealogies of Jesus are given in the New Testament. The genealogy in Luke, somewhat different from that in Matthew, apparently describes the blood line of the virgin mother, Mary. It begins, "Jesus . . . being (as was supposed) the son of Joseph, which [who] was the son of Heli [Mary's father]" (Luke 3:23). Matthew's genealogy traces the birth of Christ through Joseph's ancestry and concludes, "And Jacob begat Joseph, the husband of Mary, of whom [feminine *singular* pronoun] was born Jesus" (Matt. 1:16). Those who have traced the genealogy of Jesus in the Scriptures only add to the biblical evidence that Jesus was virgin-born.

In the New Testament, sixteen of the twenty-three references to Mary concern the birth of Jesus, and twelve of these occur in Luke's Gospel. Possibly Dr. Luke, a well-educated man, had the happy privilege of talking to the aging Mary and hearing these accounts from her own lips.

A Visit to the Hill Country

The angel told Mary that her cousin, Elizabeth, and the priest Zacharias, her husband, were also expecting a child born by the promise and power of God. The angel added, "For with God nothing shall be impossible!" (Luke 1:37) This information must have bolstered Mary's assurance and understanding and also pointed her in the direction of God's will. She traveled quickly to her cousin's home in the hill country of Judea.

When Mary entered the room, Elizabeth knew immediately that God had visited Mary. She exclaimed, "Blessed art thou among women, and blessed is the fruit of thy womb. And whence is this to me, that the mother of my Lord should come to me? . . . Blessed is she that believed: for there shall be a performance [fulfillment] of those things which were told her from the Lord" (Luke 1:42-43, 45).

Mary's joyous answer was, "My soul doth magnify the Lord, and my spirit hath rejoiced in God my Saviour. . . . For He that is mighty hath done to me great things and holy is His name" (Luke 1:46-47, 49). Mary's quietness of spirit was apparent, as were her admirable self-control, her devout attitude toward God, and her understanding of His promises to Israel.

With Elizabeth, Mary enjoyed days of fellowship and personal comfort, finding a motherly mentor who trained the young girl in the arts of motherhood.

Zacharias, having also received a message from an angel, must have been an available, though silent, friend and confidant to Mary.

Mary stayed with Elizabeth and Zacharias about three months, and after she returned, she probably told Joseph immediately about her pregnancy. It must have been a heartbreaking scene, with Joseph unable to believe her story.

When the angel had appeared to her, Mary had questioned in surprise, "How can this be, seeing I know not a man?" (Luke 1:34) She was a young girl and not sure of herself in the face of such tremendous prospects.

Joseph's turn had come to ask, "How can this thing be?" If he had been responsible, he would have known it. Joseph evidently loved Mary deeply, but that did not make it easier for a Jew of deep religious convictions to accept her incredible story. Nothing like this had ever happened before, and Joseph felt he had to face reality. Wrongfully, he decided that he would privately "put her away"—that is, break the engagement (and an engagement in those days was considered as fully binding as marriage). In all honesty, he had to disclaim the unborn child, but he would not put Mary to public shame and punishment as an adulteress.

At about that time, an angel also came to Joseph with a message from God: "Fear not to take unto thee Mary [as] thy wife, for that which is conceived in her is of the Holy Ghost" (Matt. 1:20). Then Joseph believed God and obediently took Mary as his wife.

Though Joseph dealt kindly with Mary, the neighbors probably thought exactly what she feared they did. She may still have faced scorn and slander in the community and suffered considerable embarrassment.

Bethlehem and Beyond

Then Caesar Augustus, a pagan emperor far away in Rome, decreed a census in Palestine. Joseph and Mary, being of the lineage of David (though only the man's ancestry counted in that day), were forced to go to Bethlehem to be taxed. Legend has it that she rode a shaggy donkey, but they were so poor they may not even have been able to afford one. She may have walked every trudging step of the way.

When they arrived at Bethlehem, hoping for rest and a bit of comfort, they went from inn to inn, from house to house, seeking lodging. Every hostel was full; townspeople had plans of their own; they were all very busy.

Well! you may think indignantly, *if I had lived there it would have been different. I would have done something wonderful for them!* I'm afraid such assertions are as much out of place as was Peter's when he protested to the Lord, "All the rest may forsake You, but I'm going to stick with You to the end if it kills me!" (See Matt. 26:33, 35.) For Peter was the first one to deny his Lord.

It is easy for us to look back, knowing about Jesus' miracles, death, and resurrection, sit in a comfortable church, and say what we would have done in such an emergency. We would have done then precisely what we are doing now. What are we doing about the people around us who need clothes and food and help? "Inasmuch as ye have done it unto one of the least of these My brethren," Jesus said, "ye have done it unto Me" (Matt. 25:40).

Never was a family in more unfortunate circumstances than Joseph and Mary when they entered Bethlehem. Far from home and friends, they had no one to help them. There was no attending physician. Swaddling clothes was the best gift they had for the expected Baby.

It demanded tremendous faith for this young mother to believe what God's messenger had promised her. She was so childlike that she accepted the angel's word and surely so womanlike that she wished for something far better than a stable for her Child, God's only Son and Mary's own flesh and blood.

Shepherds came out of the fields nearby, claiming they had seen angels in the night sky who directed them to the One born in the stable and sang, "Glory to God in the highest, and on earth peace, good will toward men" (Luke 2:14).

Later, wise men arrived with their gold and frankincense and myrrh, telling of the marvelous star they had followed from the East. Luke 2:19 states that "Mary kept all these things, and pondered them in her heart." This reveals a worshipful Jewish woman, modest and devout. She was an object of divine grace and her faith was a gift of God, but none of these qualities made her unique—only her Son.

The meaning of the Virgin Birth is that God is with us, that eternal deity became flesh and dwelt among us. He was truly a man, subject to temptations, trials, and sorrows just as any other man. In fact, He Himself was the perfect representative of all mankind.

Amazing beyond all human description was the fact that in a Child of flesh, God came down from heaven. How could the omnipotent God of the universe have been willing to imprison Himself in human flesh, subject to dirt, pain, tears, hunger, hate? The mind-boggling truth of the Incarnation is that Jesus, God's Son, God Himself as one of the Trinity, lay breathing in that manger-cradle.

The angel had addressed Mary, "Hail, thou that art highly favored, the Lord is with thee: blessed art thou among women" (Luke 1:28). And Elizabeth had echoed it, "Blessed art thou among women" (Luke 1:42). Yet Mary may have found it difficult at times to remember and believe that promise.

When Joseph and Mary presented the Child in the temple, Simeon exulted, "Lord...mine eyes have seen Thy salvation, which Thou hast prepared before the face of all people" (Luke 2:29-31). Simeon also prophesied that this Child would be "a sign spoken against" (Luke 2:34). That prediction has come true. Of all Bible doctrines, the Virgin Birth has probably been singled out for more ridicule and opposition than any other.

Obedience marked Mary's life, but she was no paragon of complete understanding as a mother. When her Son was twelve and stayed behind in the temple at Jerusalem, she became irritated and seemed to forget His heavenly origin: "Son, why hast Thou thus dealt with us? Behold, Thy father and I have sought Thee sorrowing" (Luke 2:48).

"Wist [understand] ye not that I must be about My Father's business?" He answered in obvious rebuke (Luke 2:49).

At the wedding feast in Cana, Mary overrode her Son's lack of consent when He said, in effect, "That concerns you, not Me. My hour has not yet come" (see John 2:4). She commanded the servants, "Whatsoever He says unto you, do it" (John 2:5). Mary knew that when Jesus undertook to solve a problem, it was always solved.

Later, when Jesus was preaching at Capernaum, Mary and some of His half-brothers came from Nazareth and could not reach Him for the crowd. When He was sent word, He said, "My mother and My brethren are these which hear the word of God, and do it" (Luke 8:21). His work was in the spiritual realm, and for Him, physical and social relationships deserved no priority.

If today Mary remains in some respects a mystery, she would not have thought of herself that way, nor would her contemporaries. Behind the fearless assertiveness of Jesus and the severe and authoritative writing of His brothers, James and Jude, there could have been no weak and passive upbringing in that home. Mary was a trusting and accepting young girl, but life must have tempered her into a strong woman without damaging her implicit faith in God.

She remained with her Son to the end. Alongside John, the beloved disciple, Mary stood near the cross when Jesus was crucified.

Simeon had spoken to Mary, over the head of the Baby Jesus, "A sword shall pierce through thy own soul also" (Luke 2:35). Surely it did there at Calvary! She had suffered in the birth of Christ. She had suffered during His life, and now she suffered in His death. Even in that suffering, there was a healing closeness. On the cross, He was suffering for His own mother, and there He comforted her, as well as substituted for her. From the cross, even as He was dying, He provided for her.

To His disciple John, Jesus gave this commission, "Behold thy mother," and to her, "Behold thy son" (see John 19:26-27). Then John, tradition has it, took her to his own house and provided for her the rest of her life. He didn't have to, but he loved Jesus enough to do it for Him.

Sometimes we lose touch with the reality of spiritual things. We become so wrapped up in our material world that we forget the intangibles of life. We feel that the more we possess, the better off we are. Yet John became a better man because he did what Jesus asked him to do. (The woman who broke the alabaster box and anointed the Lord's head with its precious contents became a better woman because she did what her heart told her to do [Mark 14:3].)

It happens with all of us. The church makes a plea for foreign or home missions, saying, "Do it for their sake." But rather, we should do it for *our own* sakes. If we do not, God will raise up others. Let us serve the Lord while we can!

A Servant at Heart

Where is Mary when the Bible last mentions her? In the first chapter of the Book of Acts her name is listed among those faithful followers of the risen Christ who prayed, believed, and waited for Pentecost. She did not attain any position of power or authority among the disciples. She, along with all the rest, looked only to her Son. And they were rewarded with the infilling of the Holy Spirit—Mary no more and no less than the others.

The psalmist wrote something that seems to describe Mary: "Behold, as the eyes of servants look unto the hand of their masters, and as the eyes of a maiden unto the hand of her mistress; so our eyes wait upon the Lord our God" (Ps. 123:2). Mary, along with many other servants of God, worked unobtrusively, accepting the suffering without bitterness and receiving its reward in purity of soul. This servanthood becomes akin to priesthood in that it required a special kind of dedication, something Mary demonstrated throughout her life.

In answering the angel, Mary described her own position very precisely: "Behold the handmaid of the Lord; be it unto me according to thy word" (Luke 1:38). We must not place Mary next to the Trinity, because mankind comes into fellowship with God only through Jesus Christ, God's Son. Mary herself praised God in what is called her Magnificat: "My spirit hath rejoiced in God my Saviour" (Luke 1:47). She accepted her Son as her Saviour. We have no need to seek the intercession of another. The heart of Jesus is always open to all who call on Him.

The early church preached preeminently the resurrection of Jesus Christ. Jesus came forth from the grave. He became victor over death! He is alive forevermore!

Mary would be the first to testify, "I have no right to adoration." For it was she who sang, rejoicing that God "hath regarded the low estate of His handmaiden: for, behold, from henceforth all generations shall call me blessed" (Luke 1:48).

3 His Miraculous Birth

Luke 2:7

When Jesus Christ began His public ministry, a Jew named Matthew was working for the Romans as a tax collector. A clerical man, he was conversant with the tax procedure of those days, which kept track of people by their families and ancestors rather than by Social Security numbers. Later, Jesus called Matthew to be His disciple. After the Lord's ascension, Matthew wrote out most carefully the narrative as he had received impressions from the Holy Spirit.

Matthew began his account of the life of Jesus Christ with a genealogy which is evidently that of Joseph, Jesus' foster father. Luke put it, in literal translation, "Jesus . . . being by legal adoption the son of Joseph" (see Luke 3:23).

People might have difficulty believing the stupendous story of Jesus, Matthew realized. After the genealogy, which traced Jesus' legal descent through Joseph back to Abraham, Matthew inserted an explanatory sentence: "Now, the birth of Jesus Christ was on this wise [like this]" (Matt. 1:18).

What Matthew had to relate was so startling and

magnificent that he wanted the full and credulous attention of his readers. His whole story of the One born to be King depended on their acceptance of his account of Jesus' birth. If Jesus were not truly born the Son of God, the Crucifixion could be nothing more than a tragedy among many tragedies of history. The Resurrection would be beyond belief.

Paul wrote, in his triumphant resurrection chapter, "If Christ be not raised, your faith is vain; ye are yet in your sins" (1 Cor. 15:17). Unless Christ rose from the dead, there is no victory over the grave. If we have believed in a miraculous resurrection and there is no resurrection, there is no hope at all! What creed is worth subscribing to which does not affirm that Jesus was the divinely conceived, unique Son of God?

The testimony of many that He was born the divine King sent from God, the evidence of His sinless life, and the circumstances of His death and resurrection assure us that we have every reason in the world to believe in His virgin birth.

While we are considering His birth in Bethlehem, let us also remember that it was not His beginning: He existed as the only begotten Son of God before the creation of the earth. In His high priestly prayer to God in John 17:24, He prayed, "Father . . . Thou loved Me before the foundation of the world."

The first verse of the Bible uses the word *God* in the plural, indicating involvement of the whole Trinity, the Godhead, in creating the heavens and the earth. Even before the earth was formed, Jesus was the eternal Word of God. Incarnation was simply the method God chose to enter the world to save mankind. The birth of Jesus has been recognized as the watershed of history. "He who in eternity rested upon the bosom of a Father without a mother," wrote the late Dr. M.E. Dodd, "in time rested upon the bosom of a mother without a father."

Heaven Came Down

Jesus' life in this world began with a miraculous birth. His ministry was characterized by miracles. His time on earth ended with the miracles of His resurrection and ascension. We worship a miracle-working God.

We cannot discuss the birth of Jesus without using the word *miraculous*. There is no other word that describes it so exactly. To call it simply a supernatural birth is not sufficient. Isaac had a supernatural birth; Abraham and Sarah, his parents, were far past the age of having children. John the Baptist had a supernatural birth too. But the word *supernatural* does not apply to the virgin birth of Jesus Christ.

Why is it difficult to believe that God could arrange a miraculous conception? Everything that exists is a miracle of God. God Himself is a miracle. The "sublimest statement in any language" is found in Genesis 1:1: "In the beginning God." The bodies in which we live are remarkable. The psalmist exclaimed, "I am fearfully and wonderfully made" (Ps. 139:14). It was a miracle when God "formed man of the dust of the ground" (Gen. 2:7). He created a beautifully functioning physical body in which human life could be tabernacled.

How dare we say that it is not reasonable or possible for God to perform a miracle in creating another human body without natural generation? What is a miracle? A miracle is an act contrary to the laws of nature as we understand them. But do we have all understanding? Does mankind possess all knowledge? Of course not! There are many unknowables in life.

We need go back only one generation to demonstrate this. Some years ago it would have been thought incredible that a man could talk into a microphone and people behind closed doors far away, or traveling down a broad highway in a speeding car, could hear his voice clearly. Our great grandfathers would have commented concerning those who prophesied such a possibility, "What utter fools!"

To claim that one could record words on a tape, store it on a shelf until years later, then put it on a machine, and have the voice still sound clear and recognizable would have been considered folly by our ancestors. They would have jibed, "What a wild fancy!"

If many of us, when children, had been told that one day we would not only be able to hear a human voice across thousands of miles, but to see happenings on the other side of the world, our reaction would have been, "Impossible!"

Perhaps one day the world may learn even more of the secrets of God's universe. But let us understand that we serve a miracle-working God who created that universe. He is never behind the times—though our conception of Him may be—because to Him there is no time. He knows not only the past and present but also the future that seems so vague to us.

The birth of Christ, though prophesied by many in minute detail, was miraculous and mysterious. We simply cannot understand it. One who had no earthly father and no heavenly mother was born of a young woman in Bethlehem, the city of David.

Bethlehem means "house of bread." He who was the Bread of Life was born in the house of bread. Yet Bethlehem made no room for the Bread of Life sent from God. "And she [Mary] brought forth her firstborn son, and wrapped Him in swaddling clothes, and laid Him in a manger, because there was no room for them in the inn" (Luke 2:7).

Luke, the writer of the third Gospel, was a physician. Surely no one would have more difficulty believing Mary's story than a medical man like Luke. Yet he gave the genealogy of Jesus' mother. He traced by inspiration, in tremendous detail, the birth of Jesus, the God-Man.

Immanuel, God with Us

When I consider the mysterious birth of our Saviour, the profoundest trouble I have is not *how*, but *why*? It is easier to understand *how* God could do it than to understand *why* God would do it. We are awed before the Incarnation. "And the Word was made flesh, and dwelt among us," John declared (John 1:14). Jesus came down to earth from heaven's glory.

> *One day when heaven was filled with His praises,*
> *One day when sin was as black as could be,*
> *Jesus came forth to be born of a virgin,*
> *Dwelt among men, my example is He!*
>
> *One day they led Him up Calvary's mountain,*
> *One day they nailed Him to die on the tree;*
> *Suffering anguish, despised and rejected:*
> *Bearing our sins, my Redeemer is He!*
>
> *Living, He loved me; dying, He saved me;*
> *Buried, He carried my sins far away;*
> *Rising, He justified freely forever:*
> *One day He's coming—O glorious day!*
>
> —J. Wilbur Chapman

Why should He? The only time the word *Immanuel* occurs in the New Testament is in Matthew's narrative (Matt. 1:23; cf. Isa. 8:8). The Hebrew means

"God with us." In his incredible announcement, the angel declared that God is no longer far away—He is *with us*!

"God's in His heaven: All's right with the world," wrote Robert Browning. I appreciate his poetry and like these lines. But if God had remained only in heaven, nothing could be right with the world. For God did not limit Himself to His own abode. Immanuel, "God with us," came down to walk on earth in the body of a man. Jesus hungered; He thirsted; He suffered. Life is bearable because it is shareable with God. We need to realize that the same Immanuel, the same God who came down to us in that lowly stable, is with us still.

When we celebrate His birth each December, after the cards are read, the packages opened, and the tree dismantled, Christmas is over. But hope's birthday goes on forever: "God with us!" Isaiah's Immanuel, identified as Jesus Christ our Lord, will never leave us. "[When] I depart, I will send Him [the Holy Spirit] unto you" (John 16:7). He will be with us all the while, "For He hath said, 'I will never leave thee, nor forsake thee' " (Heb. 13:5). God stays with us forever. "God with us" is the Good News of the Gospel.

Not many people in Bethlehem were conscious of what happened that blessed night when God came down. As far as they were concerned, nothing important occurred. Probably a few of them heard the cry of an infant, but if someone had remarked, "Messiah is born," they would have shrugged their shoulders in disbelief.

God was born into the world, though the world was unaware of it. Jesus later died physically and was buried physically. But His spirit, which could not die, picked up that dead body and transformed it to life forever. "God *is* a Spirit," Jesus revealed to the woman at the well, "and they that worship Him must worship Him in spirit and in truth" (John 4:24). Yet Isaiah prophesied that, incredible as it may seem, God's promised deliverer would be called Immanuel (Isa. 7:14).

Many people today also ignore the divine meaning of the drama of Bethlehem: "Immanuel—God with us!" He is with us still; He is by our side. One of the Trinity, a member of the Godhead, He is omnipotent, omnipresent, and eternal, yet He limited Himself in time and space. Triumphant and glorious deity, He identified Himself with His people on earth. We are told by the Apostle Paul, "He [God] hath chosen us in Him [Christ] before the foundation of the world" (Eph. 1:4).

His advent was foretold by prophets. His birth was announced by angels. His life was described by the Gospels. His purity was undeniable; He met temptation and conquered Satan. He endured death but arose again in a body of flesh and bone, and now He lives forever.

In the crises of life, one person often comforts another with "God knows." It is not an idle phrase— God *does* know! My loved one may be dead—God knows! His beloved Son was nailed to a cross. My loved one has been condemned by others. God knows! Fever? God knows! Sweat in a carpenter's shop? God knows! Hunger and thirst? God knows!

A Constant Reminder

"Immanuel" is a name we should use more often to remind ourselves that God is with us still. He is with us now in the presence of Jesus Christ in our midst— the lily of the valley, the bright and morning star, the fairest of 10,000.

We ought to be as fully interested in that birth

2,000 years ago as were the shepherds who were amazed by the angels' proclamation of Good News. "For unto you is born this day in the city of David a Saviour, which is Christ the Lord" (Luke 2:11). If Jesus were not the virgin-born Son of God, then He could not be the Son of God at all. And if He were not the Son of God, He could not be our sinless Saviour and we would have no savior at all!

By faith we come and affirm with Matthew, "Now the birth of Jesus Christ was on this wise": He became "God with us." God's voice spoke from heaven declaring, "This is My beloved Son, in whom I am well pleased" (Matt. 3:17).

Down the centuries Jesus Christ has walked with His people. He is near and dear to us even now in a manner He could not be to those who stood around the manger, in which He lay, and worshiped the newborn Child.

4 His Preparation in Childhood

Luke 2:49

A baby is appealing, helpless, and lovable. But Jesus Christ was not born to remain a baby. Sentimentalists may like to picture Him as an infant, sleeping in a manger in Bethlehem. As long as He is only a baby, they can celebrate Christ's birthday and then disregard Him the rest of the year. What can a helpless, newborn baby have to do with our daily lives?

The recorded Gospels do not spend much time with the Baby Jesus. Matthew gives two chapters and Luke three—each including a genealogy. Mark and John begin with the baptism of Christ.

His growth into manhood is covered by a certain silence. We are given one glimpse of Him when He was twelve years old. Then we do not see Him again until He appeared at the Jordan asking baptism from John the Baptist. His life in the years between is unrecorded; we call them the "hidden years" of the Master.

"The most wonderful thing about the hidden years," one has rightfully written, "is that nothing wonderful was written about them." Nevertheless,

His growing-up years were not hidden away from life. They encompassed many experiences which, if written down, would reveal many truths we would like to know about Jesus. Only one-tenth of His life is recorded; about nine-tenths of it is not.

A modern axiom goes, "Publicity is the lifeblood of success." We feel that unless a person's life has considerable exposure, unless his public relations are well-planned and his publicity well-timed, his career can never get off the ground. But the truth of the matter is that most of the greatness in any life is prepared during unknown and silent years. Jesus lived almost thirty quiet years in Nazareth before He began His ministry.

Jesus spent His first several years as what we would call today a "refugee child." He was taken before birth from the city of His conception because His mother and Joseph had to travel from Nazareth to Bethlehem for Rome's taxation.

Then, warned by an angel, Joseph quickly fled with Mary and her Child into Egypt because of Herod's attempt on the Child's life. "Out of Egypt have I called My Son" (Matt. 2:15, cf. Hosea 11:1) was the word of prophecy. After the death of Herod the Great, Joseph and Mary returned to Nazareth with the Child and there He grew to manhood.

At Home in Nazareth

A little town is a good university in which to study human nature. Nazareth held many kinds of people: Jews, Romans, Phoenicians, and other nationalities. That Jesus carefully studied people is obvious in His preaching.

Nazareth was a despised town with a bad reputation all its own. Nathanael reflected the known reputation of the town when he asked his friend, Philip,

"Can there any good thing come out of Nazareth?" (John 1:46) It was not isolated; it was by no means a remote area untouched by the world. The young Jesus heard the *tramp, tramp* of Roman legions marching through. He knew the dismay of hearing a Roman soldier's command, "Here, boy, carry my pack!" as it was thrown into the lap of a Jewish lad. He was acquainted with the mainstream of commerce that thronged the crossroads of Nazareth.

In nineteenth-century America, Horace Greeley gave a piece of wise advice to those who sought success: "Go west, young man, go west." But in the days of Josephus, the Jewish historian, there was another saying: "If you want wealth, go north. If you want wisdom, go south." Nazareth—in fact, all of Palestine—was considered "south" from the centers of culture in Greece and Rome.

Jesus did not grow up in a peaceful backwater of life. Nazareth was a rough neighborhood. Yet the town's surrounding countryside had many quiet places in which Jesus could study nature and commune with His heavenly Father, away from the bustle of the carpentry shop.

God sent His Son to be raised in a human family headed by the foster father, Joseph, in Nazareth, fulfilling the prophecy that the deliverer of Israel should be called a Nazarene (see Matt. 2:23).

Certainly we would like to know more about Jesus' "hidden years." What kind of home did He live in?

The words of Jesus show a thorough knowledge of family life. He spoke often of the children playing games in the marketplace. He was familiar with hungry children begging bread: "If his son ask bread, will he give him a stone?" (Matt. 7:9) Jesus understood the plight of widowhood, for when He went to the temple He remarked about the widow who gave all she had (Mark 12:44). Jesus always spoke a word of kindness for those who bore the problems, the heaviness, the burdens of life.

Jesus said, "Suffer little children, and forbid them not, to come unto me: for of such is the kingdom of heaven" (Matt. 19:14). He understood that even small children have been exposed to the hardships of life. Again and again His words implied what Paul wrote succinctly, "Children, obey your parents in the Lord: for this is right" (Eph. 6:1).

Jesus was never ashamed of His home and heritage or the sacrifices His parents had made. Such ungratefulness is ungodly. For every goodness that enters our lives we can turn our minds back in tender memories to all that has been done for us, treasuring the little bits of advice, the sacred moments, the pat on the hand, the strong arm on the shoulder. Jesus recognized these valid human relationships.

Jesus realized what it was to have a humble home. Probably no home anywhere in our community is more poverty-stricken than was Jesus' home. A one-room house, it had no beds, only sleeping pads that were rolled out at night. People slept in the garments they wore and rolled their cloaks around them for covers. Usually there were no fireplaces inside the houses.

The father or the eldest son would lead in thanksgiving before and after each meal—probably not more than two meals a day. What did they have to thank God for? Often there was little rice for the bowl, little flour for the bread, little oil for the lamps. Their lives would be considered destitute by our standards today.

Many people never owned a change of garments; they had only what they were wearing, ragged though it might have been. If we have worn hand-medowns, we remember how we longed for something new of our own. Most of these people never even hoped for that. They sensed they would never have anything they could call their own except misery, burdens, and sin.

At Home in the Temple

God's Word reaches into the silent years of Jesus' youth and gives us only one glimpse of Him. We see the Child Jesus at twelve years of age, with His family, going down to the Holy City, Jerusalem. Probably a whole group of relatives made the journey together.

A Jewish lad was required to attend the temple three times during his childhood. On the eighth day of life, he was circumcised (see Luke 2:21). Thirty-three days later he was taken for presentation to the Lord, especially if he was a firstborn male (Ex. 13:12), and a sacrifice culminating the mother's days of purification was offered at that time (Luke 2:22-24). When a Jewish boy was about twelve, he would again go to the temple to become officially "a son of the Law." It was a thrilling ceremony to participate in, the first time a boy accompanied his father to worship God.

Approaching the Holy City, the travelers could see the gleaming dome of the temple. The men and boys usually walked together and the women came behind more slowly, bringing the necessary camping equipment. Often more than half a million Jews came to the city of Jerusalem for the festivals. There were no inns to take care of them all. Some, of course, had relatives who would crowd them into their homes. The family from Nazareth would have had no shekels to pay, even if there had been hotels.

Later, Jesus talked about buying five sparrows for two farthings; this was the kind of marketing He had known. The cheapest thing that was offered—this was their daily fare. The Bible indicates that the common people heard Him gladly. Of course! He was one of them. "The Spirit of the Lord is upon Me," Jesus said, "because He hath anointed Me to preach the Gospel to the poor" (Luke 4:18).

Surely the Boy Jesus felt an awesome, sacred joy in His heart on reaching maturity as "a son of the Law." More than likely, He had received religious instruction by the local teachers of the Law. All His life He had been memorizing the Scriptures as required. Jewish parents had been commanded, "Thou shalt teach them [these words] diligently unto thy children" (Deut. 6:7).

As Jesus visited the temple, He was anxious to observe all the ceremonies. First, the sacrifices were offered. Then the Sanhedrin, the teachers of the Law, rather than holding their deliberations in private, this one day a year came outside and held their meeting in public—not out in the public court amid the noise of the outside world, the bleating of animals, and the clanking of the money changers, but in the temple forum, the public auditorium, so to speak. All who desired could sit and listen to them. So Jesus did.

He became so fascinated that when His relatives had paid their respects, done their duty, and left, He didn't go with them. He didn't intend to disobey, but He was completely absorbed. His entire being was given to this House of God, His true home. This was His realm; the leaders of His people were discussing His Father's affairs. The fact that day and night passed meant nothing to Him. His calendar was eternity.

In the meantime, Mary and Joseph started home to Nazareth, traveling in different companies. Sometime later, they noticed Jesus was missing. They passed a fearful night and hurried back to Jerusalem.

Jesus had been in the temple all the time. Because Jesus knew all things, some think that He was picking the teachers to pieces, asking brash questions. Not at all! He was behaving in a reverent manner, drinking in the words He heard from the teachers, and asking honest questions. The Bible records that the teachers of the Law were amazed at His depth of understanding. He wasn't trying to trick them; He wasn't telling them; He was listening attentively. They were amazed at a twelve-year-old boy being so interested. Why wasn't He playing with the other boys?

This was an hour He had waited for. There must have been times when He asked Mary and Joseph questions they couldn't answer. They may have replied, "Son, when you go to the temple, you can ask the priests. The scribes will be able to tell you." Now Jesus was making up for lost time. This was a momentous time in His life.

When Jesus' mother and Joseph finally found Him, they must have been relieved, yet upset.

"Don't You know we've been worried about You?" Mary asked, like any concerned mother would.

"And He said unto them, 'How is it that ye sought Me? Wist [understand, know] ye not that I must be about My Father's business?' " (Luke 2:49) In other words, "Don't you understand how important this is to Me? I must tend to My Father's business!" This was the first of a series of "musts" in the Master's life.

At Home with His Mission

Here and there we learn about other of Jesus' habits. On the Sabbath He always went to the Lord's house, for the Bible mentions, "as His custom was" (Luke 4:16). He was no doubt a prayerful boy. He learned the prayers of children from His mother and from hearing Joseph pray.

Jesus must have learned the Scriptures from the rabbis, because He quoted from Old Testament literature quite often. What we understand about His early life reveals His sense of mission, even as a youth.

Jesus was surely a deep thinker. It is incorrect to take for granted that a person who works with his hands never thinks. What He was doing may have become so mechanical and His fingers may have grown so methodically skillful that His mind was able to turn to other matters.

One of the best Bible teachers I ever knew was an unlettered man who had no formal training. There was no church in his community, and services were held in the schoolhouse on Sunday mornings twice a month. But Sunday evenings this man would sit down with his family and the Word of God. They would read it together and go over the Sunday School lesson for the next Lord's Day. All week long, as this man worked, he would turn that lesson over in his mind and ask God to prepare his heart with wisdom. He was a thinking and a praying man, and he had vast influence for God in his community.

Jesus was blessed with a heritage of godliness and hard work in His home. Work became the habit of His life. Luke wrote, "Jesus increased in wisdom and stature, and in favor with God and man" (Luke 2:52). The only perfect person who ever lived in all the world was Jesus Christ. He is our pattern. He was a normal boy—but more. He was God's perfect example, a volume in one sentence.

He increased in wisdom; that is our mental pattern.

He increased in stature—He grew up. The Bible seems to teach us here that He had a strong body and that He cared for the physical endowments God gave Him. He did not indulge in habits or pastimes He knew would bring weakness to His body.

He gained favor—first of all with God, in His spiritual growth; then also with other people. People are not made to live alone; children are born social beings. It is up to us as parents to train them, not only at home, but in the community. How else can they learn to live in this hectic world?

Why did God give us only this one picture of Jesus out of almost thirty years of His life? I have no idea. But I do know that that one picture depicts Jesus at "church."

This is the pattern God wants all parents to remember in training their children. And if children remember only one truth about Jesus as a child, they should remember what happened at the temple, where He sought to understand more of His Father's business.

5 His Authenticating Miracles

Acts 2:22

On the Day of Pentecost, Peter proclaimed of his Saviour, "Jesus of Nazareth, a man approved of God among you by miracles and wonders and signs, which God did by Him in the midst of you, as ye yourselves also know" (Acts 2:22). If we believe in an all-powerful God, we must believe in miracles.

When Nicodemus approached Jesus, he confessed, "No man can do these miracles that Thou do, except God be with him" (John 3:2). Nicodemus believed Jesus was sent from God because of the credentials He showed—the power to perform miracles.

Yet a few challenged Jesus' source of power, accusing Him of doing mighty works by the power of the devil. Today, as in the first century, each man has to decide for himself the source of Jesus' power.

What is a miracle? A wonderful, unexpected occurrence can be a miracle. Something supernatural is a miracle, or an unusual power or sign. The fact that Jesus was a miracle-worker made Him unique.

We believe that God can work miracles without violence to His nature or to His creation. But two important questions are, "Does God always count as miraculous the things we regard as miraculous? Or would what we consider a miracle and what God considers a miracle be proverbial horses of a different color?" Sometimes we recount as a miracle some combination or timing of naturally caused circumstances that might or might not reflect the supernatural intervention of God.

We comprehend so little about the unlimited power of God. We can only view His miracle-power in action as we read of the many strange reversals of natural forces recorded in both the Old and New Testaments. During Jesus' ministry, He performed at least thirty-five miracles described in the Gospels. Jesus Christ demonstrated the power of God that men might know that He came from God. "And many other signs truly did Jesus..." wrote the Apostle John, "but these are written that ye might believe that Jesus is the Christ, the Son of God" (John 20:30-31).

To begin with, the birth of Jesus was a miraculous event, never known to mankind before or since. His public ministry was also marked by miracles. Yet Jesus never performed a miracle for His own benefit or convenience or to excite the curious crowds. He refused to transform stones into bread to feed Himself, and He refused to perform a miracle to entertain Herod. His purpose was to alleviate the suffering of mankind and to present credentials of His deity and proof of His sympathy.

Even the Winds and the Sea Obey Him
The miracles of Jesus were impressive because men have always had a healthy respect for power. His miracle-working power was demonstrated in the realms of nature, physical healing, and resurrection.

We recognize that the forces of nature have awesome power, that the gently falling raindrops can become a surging flood, that the gentle winds can become a destructive tornado funnel. A TV commercial has coined the expression, "It's not nice to fool Mother Nature!" The God of the universe asserts His power and strength through natural forces. If He counteracts the forces of His creation, that is a miracle.

When Christ stilled the storm on the Sea of Galilee, immediately there came an amazing calm. "What manner of man is this," the disciples marveled, "that even the winds and the sea obey Him?" (Matt. 8:27).

The first recorded evidence of His unusual power was at the wedding in Cana. To please His mother, to increase the joy of the social occasion, and to give confidence to His freshman disciples, He compressed nature's processes into an instant to turn water into excellent wine. "When the ruler of the feast had tasted the water that was made wine . . . [he] called the bridegroom and said unto him, . . . 'Thou hast kept the good wine until now' " (John 2:9-10).

Jesus also multiplied food, using a boy's lunch and a few disciples to help Him feed thousands. Again His provision was bountiful: "And they did eat, and were all filled, and there was taken up of fragments that remained to them twelve baskets" (Luke 9:17).

Most of us have prayed that somewhere, sometime, the Lord Jesus would pick us up like that and use us in being part of a modern miracle. We ask Him to take what little we have and make much of it.

Jesus Christ walked on water to reach His storm-tossed disciples, calling to them, "Be of good cheer; it is I; be not afraid." Peter blurted out, "Lord, if it be Thou, bid me come unto Thee on the water. . . . And when Peter was come down out of the ship, he walked on the water, to go to Jesus" (Matt. 14:27-29). The response of the disciples to this incident was, "Of a truth Thou art the Son of God" (Matt. 14:33).

This matchless Son of God could wither a fig tree with a word or call fish to do His bidding. After His resurrection, His discouraged disciples went fishing and all that night they caught nothing. In the morning, He appeared on the shore and challenged them to try throwing their nets once again. At once He rewarded their faith with full nets (John 21:6).

Christ's followers beheld this and many more evidences of His unusual power, the power of God controlling nature.

The Great Physician's Touch

Jesus could also control natural forces affecting one's body. The hymnwriter celebrated His power to heal in the familiar words, "The Great Physician now is near, the sympathizing Jesus."

The threefold ministry of Jesus was teaching, healing, and preaching. Twenty-five of His miracles were performed to help and heal people. Our Lord responded to the suffering about Him. In His miracles, as nowhere else but the Cross, we focus on His kind heart bared to a lost world.

Today science refers to certain medical laboratory discoveries as "miracle drugs." Some scientists realize that men are only beginning to discover the remedies God has provided in His creation and are far more tolerant toward the idea of a miracle-working God and the biblical accounts of miracles. The Great Physician may continue to uncover healing powers previously unknown to us.

Personally, it is much easier for me to accept God's explanations than to trust the scientific theories of men. If I am willing to admit that man can discover a miracle drug, with no difficulty at all I can believe in a miracle-working God.

The crippled man at the pool of Bethesda said, "I have no man ... to put me into the pool," but Jesus became that man and healed him, saying "Rise, take up thy bed, and walk" (John 5:7-8).

On another occasion, Jesus met ten lepers who cried out, "Jesus, Master, have mercy on us" (Luke 17:13). He healed them and they departed with rejoicing. Only one returned "and with a loud voice glorified God, and fell down on his face at His feet, giving Him thanks" (Luke 17:15-16).

Blind Bartimaeus cried out the prayer of the helpless, "Jesus, Thou Son of David, have mercy on me!" and Jesus showed miraculous mercy: "Go thy way; thy faith hath made thee whole" (Mark 10:47, 52).

When all other doctors had failed, the Great Physician healed the hemorrhaging woman "with an issue of blood." She dared to reach out and touch His garment. "Who touched Me?" Jesus asked, calling forth her confession. "And He said unto her, 'Daughter, be of good comfort; thy faith hath made thee whole' " (Luke 8:48).

At some time, all of us have turned to God out of pressured desperation. We are prone to do everything we can before asking God for help. After we run out of ideas, after exhausting every method possible, in our failure then we cry out to God. Yet no matter how feeble our touch, Jesus always responds with care and understanding.

The miracle-working power of Jesus reaches across the centuries and makes the difference between living and merely existing. This was part of His purpose in coming to earth.

Christ was born by a miracle, performed miracles, and the miracle of Easter morning is why Christians are living and singing now rather than existing in frustration. The realization of His power in us puts purpose into all we do.

The natural result of this loving, healing power should have been, it seems, applause from the Galilean and Judean crowds. They should have been shouting, "Our great God is moving among us!" Instead, the Pharisees and Sadducees murmured against Jesus and stirred up controversy. Instead of joy, they evidenced bitterness and persecution. The crowd wanted only entertainment and the leaders of the Jews sneered, "This fellow does not cast out devils, but by Beelzebub the prince of the devils" (Matt. 12:24).

Even John the Baptist succumbed to desperation and doubt, as each of us sometimes does in our Christian walk. He dispatched some of his followers to Jesus to ask, "Art Thou He that should come, or do we look for another?" (Matt. 11:3)

"Go and show John again those things which ye do hear and see," Jesus answered. "The blind receive their sight, and the lame walk, the lepers are cleansed, and the deaf hear, and the dead are raised up, and the poor have the Gospel preached to them. And blessed is he, whosoever shall not be offended in Me" (Matt. 11:4-5).

On the other hand, when the Pharisees asked Jesus for a sign, He replied, "An evil and adulterous generation seeks after a sign" (Matt. 12:39)—that is, a miraculous event. Men have been looking, looking, looking through the centuries. "Art Thou the One sent from God?" they still ask.

New Life Without and Within

With the end of the Apostolic Age, miracles seemed to cease. Yet since then, Christians freely admit that it took a miracle—"a miracle of love and grace"—to redeem their lives. Every time a soul is saved, every time a life is restored, a miracle occurs.

It took a miracle to give purpose to the life of the Apostle John. When John was chosen a disciple, Jesus called him and his brother James "Boanerges, which is, the sons of thunder" (Mark 3:17). We must be careful that we do not pray simply for God to make us feel good, but rather that God will make us into people who will do good. There's a vast difference.

Simon Peter vacillated back and forth in spite of the Master's words, "Thou art Peter, and upon this rock I will build My church" (Matt. 16:18). Later, Peter stood like a rock at Pentecost. It took a miracle to change Peter into a rocklike believer.

Jesus also had a purpose in raising Jairus' daughter (see Mark 5:41-42) and in restoring the widow's son at Nain (see Luke 7:11-15). Christ demonstrated the power of God in resurrection so all who saw and heard might know His deity and the loving purposes of God to restore fellowship between Himself and mankind.

The greatest miracle of resurrection, other than that of Christ Himself, occurred at a tomb in Bethany. Lazarus had been dead four days. Jesus reached into the darkness of death and summoned, "Lazarus, come forth!" (John 11:43) He came back from decay to wholeness, from death to life, from sleep to consciousness, from the beyond to the present. There was no doubt on the part of those who stood there that Lazarus had been dead; and yet, restored to life, he walked out of the tomb. It was a miracle.

The greatest miracles of all are still being worked in our time—the miracles of salvation, the new birth or regeneration. Any time a person hears and heeds the Saviour's call, "Come unto Me," and is restored to the family of the heavenly Father, that redemptive, miracle-working power of God in Jesus Christ performs a miracle that lasts forever.

6 His Unfailing Friendship

John 15:8

Many religions are built on what a man does to appease his God. But Christianity is based on what God, through His Son Jesus Christ, does for us—what He's done for us in the past, what He's doing for us in the present, and what He wishes to do for us in the future. He would like to be our Friend.

Do you want to be a friend of Jesus?

On the occasion recorded in John 15, Jesus was speaking to His disciples. He always identified Himself with His people. In the climactic part of His message Jesus said, "Ye are My friends, if ye do whatsoever I command you" (John 15:14).

Who Are Your Friends?

Concerning friendship, Solomon spoke many wise words, including, "A friend loves at all times, and a brother is born for adversity" (Prov. 17:17). But we speak of a higher and loftier friendship and brotherhood when we consider the close relationship between Jesus and ourselves. Our Lord and Saviour, who walked among us in human flesh, did everything then and is doing everything now to identify Himself as our Friend. And He wishes us to identify ourselves as His friends.

Ralph Waldo Emerson, in his essay on friendship, observed that "no advantage, no gold, no power can be a match for a friend."

In the Old Testament we are told that friendship is up to us: "A man that has friends must show himself friendly" (Prov. 18:24a). Friendship is always a reciprocal affair. In the words of the old pop song, "It Takes Two to Tango;" likewise it takes two to make a quarrel, and it also takes two to make a friendship.

An English proverb goes, "He is my friend who grinds at my mill." That is, if you are going to be my friend, there must be opportunity for me to express my friendship to you. You must permit me to do something for you. It is not enough for me to offer friendship; you are under obligation to answer.

Of course, it is possible to love someone and the love not be returned. The poets call it "unrequited love." This happens. As with human friendships, there can be no friendship with Christ as long as the love is on Christ's side only. But when love answers love, friendship is born.

George W. Truett, pastor of First Baptist Church in Dallas for forty-four years, said, "A man must keep his friendships in good repair. And he ought to count his enemies just as closely as he counts his friends."

Who are your friends? When you think about your genuine friends, you have to eliminate many acquaintances. Under difficult conditions, you would call only on certain people. Whom would you phone in the middle of the night, knowing that they would not mind being disturbed? Who would wish to be at your side if you needed them? Who would have to sense only that you wanted them—nothing else, no further explanation?

Joseph Fort Newton once wrote, "No man is useless who is a friend and no man is hopeless who has a friend."

One desperate soul who felt he had no friends wrote a note in the darkness of the night, "I'm taking the only way out of this hell of loneliness," intending to end his life. But self-destruction is not the only way out. There is an exit. Jesus gave us an alternative—His friendship.

"There is a friend that sticks closer than a brother," Solomon wrote prophetically (Prov. 18:24b). That Friend is Jesus Christ.

A Call to Friendship

Jesus talked often about the possibility of friendship with Him. "Henceforth, I call you not servants . . . I have called you friends," He assured His followers (John 15:15).

It was the night before He would face crucifixion. Judas had already left the group, and the Master craved the closeness of His loyal disciples. They were supposed to be watching with Him in the Garden of Gethsemane, yet when He sought them out, they were fast asleep. He was deeply disappointed: "What, could ye not watch with Me one hour?" (Matt. 26:40)

Nevertheless, Jesus prayed, "Holy Father, keep through Thine own name those whom Thou hast given Me" (John 17:11). Though some of those "loyal" men temporarily deserted Him in the moment of danger, nothing could change the love of Jesus toward those He counted as His friends. He never deserted one of His own.

"Greater love hath no man than this, that a man lay down his life for his friends," He said (John 15:13). This is what Jesus did for us. He counts friends as dear, and means for His people to do the same.

T. DeWitt Talmadge gave us a good recipe for keeping friends: "If someone criticizes your friend in your presence, take off twenty-five percent for exaggeration and twenty-five percent for what gossip added to it along the way; take off another twenty-five percent for the circumstances of overpowering temptation; then dismiss the other twenty-five percent because you haven't heard the other side of the story." There is no criticism left when people love as true friends.

"But isn't it true," you may ask, "that where there's smoke there's fire?" Not necessarily. If the Israelites in Egypt could make bricks without straw, the devil can surely make smoke without fire. That has always been a satanic art, and something that Christians who are supposed to be in the forgiving business need to beware.

Unfortunately, across the desk in my study I have heard, "People at work will more readily forgive me than the people at church." That may sometimes be true in experience, but it is wrong in principle. We Christians should be forgiving people because Jesus has not withheld His forgiveness from us. If you are a friend of Jesus, sit up and take notice; stand up and be counted!

Had we lived in Jesus' time, would we have been among His friends? Are we His friends now? That is the best means of deciding. Love is the strongest tie on earth. Friendships can't be bought and sold: a "you-do-for-me-and-I'll-do-for-you" relationship can't last. "Ye are My friends," Jesus said, "if you do whatsoever I command you"—*voluntarily* (John 15:14).

A servant is one who *must* be obedient to his master. A friend is one who *wishes* to serve on a *voluntary basis.* I want to be your friend, but I don't want you to *make* me be your friend.

The bond of friendship grows with exercise. In John 15, the Master was not speaking about salvation, but discipleship. He puts us to the test by saying, "If you will." That is, our wills are surrendered; His will comes first. To some it seems too high a price. That was the conclusion of the rich young ruler (see Mark 10:17-22).

In the early 1800s, a French officer started to surrender to Britain's Lord Nelson. Nelson said, "First give me your sword, and then give me your hand." But you can't force friendship. That which is easily bestowed can be easily withdrawn. A true friendship will take root and grow tall in spite of trying circumstances.

There must be mutual faith between friends. The Bible says, "Abraham believed God, and . . . he was called the friend of God" (James 2:23).

The friendship of Jonathan and David is one of the most touching in the Bible. Despite the risks, Jonathan did all that he could for David and placed no obligations on him. Though Jonathan later died in battle, as soon as David became king, he sought out the children of Jonathan and provided for his handicapped son (see 2 Sam. 9:1-13).

The Blessings of Friendship

Friendship with Jesus ushers great blessings into our lives. Any time we are bound together with another, there is strength as a result of unity. Jesus promised a reward for friendship with Him, "For all things that I have heard of My Father I have made known unto you. Ye have not chosen Me, but I have chosen you" (John 15:15b-16).

God chooses us because of His mercy and His goodness. In earthly life, Jesus did not think Himself too good to walk our streets, eat at our tables, and live in our circumstances. He was counted as a cursed Jew and a friend of sinners by the religious leaders. Yet He did not consider this unworthy of His deity and majesty. He was perfectly willing to suffer that He might be regarded as our Friend.

Without exception, Jesus was always a Friend to those who looked to Him. On Golgotha, to the thief who turned and begged, "Lord, remember me!" Jesus answered, "Today shalt thou be with Me in paradise" (Luke 23:42-43). The Lord has never turned His back on a soul. If there is any turning away, we do it. Our Lord never did and He never will.

How could we possibly count the blessings of Jesus' friendship? We will never even begin to comprehend their full scope until we see Him face to face. Then we will know even as we are known.

In the meantime, we must become used to the richness of the blessings He bestows. We need to start acting like Jesus, being like Him morally, mentally, socially—not counting ourselves above others but ministering to them in Jesus' name.

On a rooftop at Joppa, Simon Peter was instructed, in a vision, to eat of certain "unkosher" foods offered him. "Lord, it is unclean!" he protested. Jesus replied, "Don't tell Me anything that I have created is unclean. Let Me do the cleansing!" (See Acts 10:9-15.)

When Peter insisted, "Lord, you know I am Your friend," Jesus replied, "Feed My sheep" (see John 21:15-17). If we want to be His friends, then we should do what Jesus would be doing. We are to be extensions of our Friend.

If Jesus were bodily on earth today, what do you think He would be doing? Surely, He would be about His Father's business. "Feed my sheep! Feed my lambs!" He gently, but firmly, commanded Peter.

When you minister to the children of God, remember that there is a close tie between the friendship of Jesus and His special blessing on those who feed His sheep.

How meaningful is the old hymn: "What a Friend we have in Jesus, all our sins and griefs to bear!" Where else do you have such a Friend?

In His early ministry, when followers started to drift away, Jesus sadly asked His disciples, "Will ye also go away?" Simon Peter spoke for the whole group, "Lord, to whom shall we go? Thou hast the words of eternal life" (see John 6:67-69). The friendship of Jesus affords us comfort and reassurance. We can sing with the songwriter, "He walks with me, and He talks with me, and He tells me I am His own!" That is the kind of Friend Jesus is.

The Demands of Friendship

A man without friends is the poorest of all mortals, but a man who tries to a make friends on the basis of what they can give him finds only shallow relationships.

"Ye have not chosen Me," Jesus explained, "but I have chosen you, and ordained you, that ye should go and bring forth fruit, and that your fruit should remain" (John 15:16). You will never love people you don't like to begin with. Problems ensue when a person marries someone he claims to "love"—but doesn't really like. Sometimes it seems far easier to love people generally than to like them enough individually to be genuinely warm and concerned.

When Lazarus was at the point of death, Jesus' life was in danger if He should enter the Jerusalem area. His disciples asked Him, "Shall we go?"

"Our friend Lazarus is sick," Jesus answered. That was all it required for them to know what He planned. When they heard Jesus identify Lazarus as His friend, they realized He would go regardless of personal danger.

Thomas appealed to the others, "Let us also go, that we may die with Him" (John 11:16). They knew nothing would keep Jesus away, that He would go when and where He was needed.

One great story of a Christian's life is that he has a heritage of friends. Our Quaker brethren call themselves "The Society of Friends." When we meet in church as the body of Christ, this gathering ought to be a redemptive body of friends, because friends are in the restoration business. "Ye which are spiritual, restore such a one in the spirit of meekness" (Gal. 6:1).

If you go through life destroying, you have picked the devil's side. But if you are willing to go through life helping, restoring, and building up the body of Christ, you have chosen the company of Jesus. "Herein is My Father glorified, that ye bear much fruit; so shall ye be My disciples" (John 15:8).

Jesus offers us the beginning of friendship with Him. He will be with us in the bonds of friendship, and we will have the blessings of His friendship. But it has to begin in love: "This is My commandment, that ye love one another, as I have loved you" (John 15:12).

7 His Perfect Forgiveness

Ephesians 1:7

Our loving Saviour's most telling act of grace occurred while He was dying on the cross. There Jesus Christ spoke the most redemptive words of a man in flesh, words of forgiveness. Even in the agony of excruciating pain (and His body was just like ours), Jesus turned His face to heaven and prayed for His executioners: "Father, forgive them; for they know not what they do" (Luke 23:34).

Stephen, a deacon in the early church and her first martyr, followed the example of his Master: "Lord, lay not this sin to their charge" (Acts 7:60). This was not easy to do. It didn't save his life; he died brutally as the stones crushed his body. But there was the quality of heaven about his spirit, and the power of his faith was an anesthetic enabling him to say, "Father, forgive them!"

This word *forgive*—what does it mean? It is not a high, theological word. It is extremely real and pertinent in our relationships to one another. The word means "give for."

Suppose I drove an automobile from a new car lot

with a buyer's contract and then completely wrecked it—"totaled" it, as the insurance people would call it. Then suppose I had it towed back to the lot and asked the dealer, "What will you give me for it now?" His response would be obvious.

When we ask for God's forgiveness, we confess, "O God, I have totaled my life. I have made it fit for nothing but the junkyard. What will You give for it?"

The answer from God's throne of grace is, "My only begotten Son." The only One who is interested in a man who has totally wrecked his life is Jesus Christ, the Son of God.

You may protest, "I'm popular. People like me. They laugh at me and with me." But when the world quits laughing and you get off, what then? When your earthly values no longer have meaning, then what will your life be worth?

Reactions to Jesus' Parable of the Prodigal Son (Luke 15:11-32) illustrate this. People can easily identify how they feel toward the boy who demanded his father's earnings, and then went away and wasted them. Back home there was another son who understood his father even less. Finally he complained to his father, "Lo, these many years do I serve thee . . . and yet thou never gave me a kid, that I might make merry with my friends" (Luke 15:29).

"Son, don't you understand?" his father mourned, "Thou art ever with me, and all that I have is thine."

Our world today resembles that home. On many nights, the jails are filled to capacity. This is a shame. However, we might feel strongly about full jails on Saturday nights, but be indifferent about empty church pews on Sunday mornings!

From God's perspective, it is sin in both places. But we are prone to forgive what we might call "respectable sins," and not forgive the things which we deem corrupt. There is not one of us, of any age or race, who doesn't need forgiveness. Forgiveness is channeled from God as a continual flow of fresh water. If we dam it up, the source will be blocked and the thirst will go unrefreshed.

Forgive and Forget

When we pray, "Forgive us our debts," we have not finished. Jesus taught us to pray, "Forgive us our debts, *as* we forgive our debtors" (Matt. 6:12, italics added). If you feel unforgiven, if you feel depressed, if you pray for forgiveness and still do not have *forgetfulness*, maybe you stopped too soon—perhaps you prayed, "Father, forgive *my* sins," and did not pray for the one who sinned against you. The man who refuses to forgive sabotages the bridge over which he is trying to walk.

Forgiveness fosters togetherness. Jesus is the only One who can remove the divisions that exist between us: "For He is our peace, who hath made both one, and hath broken down the middle wall of partition between us; having abolished in His flesh the enmity" (Eph. 2:14-15).

If Jesus had emerged from the grave and confronted the Jewish leaders and Pilate who had condemned Him to death, He could have started the bloodiest revolution the world has ever known. But Jesus did not come to launch a physical revolution. It was a spiritual revolution which He planned: changing individual human beings by new birth from above. He might have gone to the Sanhedrin and to the governor's palace to boast, "You didn't get rid of Me; I will yet be your judge!" This was true. But Jesus did not approach His persecutors with threats.

Instead, Jesus wanted to be with His disciples who were cowering in fear and despair because they thought He was dead. Thus Jesus Christ teaches us the dynamics of forgiveness: as soon as He had opportunity, He went to comfort His disciples.

What does pardon or forgiveness involve? First, it involves a moral readjustment. We have a mental transformation; we feel differently. It also involves a spiritual emancipation; we start acting differently.

One skilled doctor repeatedly recommended to his patients that they go hear a certain minister.

"You mean go and counsel with him?"

"No, go hear him preach."

Some of the other ministers in town resented this "endorsement" and finally asked the doctor, "Why do you recommend this particular pastor?"

"Because," he explained, "I know that minister preaches forgiveness, and no one can get well if he is not willing to forgive."

Confess and Be Reconciled

The classic picture of forgiveness is seen as the Prodigal Son arrived home after squandering his inheritance. He began with confession: "Father, I have sinned."

Before there is forgiveness there must be realization of guilt. Sin is the major source of man's guilt. This can be good if it is admitted; it can be tragic if it is repressed. Guilt comes as a result of a violated conscience, the ignoring of the "inner voice" that warns us. In our time, many choose to detoxify sin by putting new labels on old poisons and new names on old evils.

The Bible speaks sharply against any person who feels he has no need of forgiveness, no need to pray. Who can look inside himself and feel that he is above sin, that he has done no wrong?

The Lord has declared that revival will not come to

any sinful people. "If My people, which are called by My name, shall humble themselves, and pray, and turn from their wicked ways; then will I hear from heaven" (2 Chron. 7:14).

Only when we recognize our true spiritual condition can we do something about it. In a Richmond, Virginia hospital where my chaplain brother was taking an internship in mental health, a man was dying. He was fidgety, irritable, and frustrated. He had been there long enough for the treatment to be making an improvement in his condition, but he knew it wasn't.

Finally the man's relatives allowed the doctors to give him the bad news: he had a terminal illness. Almost immediately, his attitude changed. He began to savor the last days of life. Instead of cursing those who waited on him, he began to thank everyone. There was reconciliation with those around him. Likewise, a man who becomes reconciled to God will also desire reconciliation with others.

Reconciliation with God is always available, as we are assured in Ephesians 2:13: "But now in Christ Jesus ye who sometimes were far off are made nigh by the blood of Christ."

And we are all by nature "far off" from God. All have sinned! Man does not live alone, and therefore he does not have the right to live a bad example before the children next door or his own, for that matter! If it is true that "all have sinned, and come short of the glory of God" (Rom. 3:23), what can we do about it?

"If we confess our sins," John wrote, "He is faithful and just to forgive us our sins, and to cleanse us from all unrighteousness" (1 John 1:9). There must be confession before we can obtain forgiveness.

Not all confession must be public; yet not all

confession can be private either. What's more, you have the right to confess your sin, but no right to confess the sin of another. Let the circle of the offenses committed be the circle of the confession made.

Secret sin should be confessed in secret. Private sin should be confessed privately, before God, because all sin is against God. When you wrong a brother, that wrong is also against the God who made that brother (see Ps. 51:4). So you must confess to God first. Then let God direct you to the wronged brother, if that is needed.

Open sin should be acknowledged openly— though not in a manner that would be harmful to one's associates or ruinous to one's character. The best way to confess openly is to, as the saying goes, "pick up the feathers of the bundle your toe opened." In other words, if you try your best to clean up the mess, that gives evidence to the whole world that you actually feel differently in your heart.

Responsible confession is thorough and open. Open living demonstrates open repentance.

"If thou bring thy gift to the altar, and remember that thy brother hath aught against thee; leave there thy gift before the altar, and go thy way; first be reconciled to thy brother, and then come and offer thy gift" (Matt. 5:23-24). If he doesn't forgive you, that becomes his burden, but you cannot worship God acceptably with an unrighted wrong on your conscience.

What if one who has wronged you does not come to you? Forgive him before he comes. If you hesitate, your prayer life will be hindered. You can't pray when you desperately need to forgive. A chip on the shoulder nurtures hate in the heart and the cancer of rebellion in the soul.

"Judge not, and ye shall not be judged," Jesus said; "condemn not, and ye shall not be condemned; forgive, and ye shall be forgiven" (Luke 6:37). Whether or not the other person ever forgives you, God will forgive you right then and there.

One ought not to speak words publicly and think he can make it right by confessing privately. There is considerable difference between the type of apology we make to man for our mistakes and the kind of confession of sin we make to the God who knows everything. He discerns our motives as well as our words and actions.

How is sin against another person a sin against God? First of all, every individual is one of God's creatures, made in His image. When he was tempted by Potiphar's wife, Joseph enunciated a pungent principle: "How then can I do this great wickedness, and sin against God?" (Gen. 39:9) Joseph understood that sin is never really private or personal—nor is it merely a triangle: two persons and God. It reaches out and affects many other people. In Joseph's case, the woman made a false accusation anyway, and it affected her husband, Potiphar, the Pharoah, and all the family of father Jacob.

Beneath the Cleansing Flood

Centuries ago, when a king of Scotland was being pursued by those who wanted his throne, he had to submerge himself in a stream of water to keep the dogs from tracking him down. There is only one stream in all this world where we can hide from the pursuing guilt of sin, and that is in the blood of Jesus Christ. At the Cross, God Himself undertook to cover our sins and to remove our transgressions. Jesus Christ is the only hiding place.

The Apostle Paul often preached in locales where

he had previously persecuted Christians and in areas where he himself had been persecuted. But he preached in the fervor of God's love and with boldness of faith—never as one who gloated over his sins. "Christ Jesus came into the world to save sinners, of whom I am chief" (1 Tim. 1:15). He wasn't claiming any merit badge. He was humbling himself before man and God and asking forgiveness. He was indicating that he himself was the ultimate proof of God's forgiveness.

Jesus Christ is the only source of forgiveness for king or peasant, man or woman, boy or girl, pew or pulpit—the only One who can cleanse our sin. It is Jesus only, "In whom we have redemption through His blood, the forgiveness of sins, according to the riches of His grace" (Eph. 1:7).

8 His Glorious Transfiguration

Mark 9:2

If we were listing the main points of Christ's biography, we would certainly include His birth, His baptism, His temptation, His crucifixion, and His resurrection. But often His transfiguration is passed over lightly because so little is recorded concerning that strange event.

It was both literally and figuratively a mountaintop experience, but we are not sure exactly which mountain! The most likely place seems to be Mount Hermon, which was about fifty miles from Nazareth and more than twice that far from Jerusalem.

The timing of the event seems crucial. The ministry of Jesus was nearly finished and the Cross loomed in the near future (see Mark 8:31). Little by little the curious crowds had left. The mammoth multitudes had dwindled away until only a few of His faithful followers remained. It was at this time that Peter made his great confession, "Thou art the Christ" (Mark 8:29); that Jesus rebuked Peter for attempting to dissuade Him from the Cross (Mark 8:33); and that Jesus proclaimed to His disciples that some of them would "not taste death, till they [had] seen the kingdom of God come with power" (Mark 9:1).

Several days later, that latter promise was fulfilled. Jesus drew His "inner circle"—Peter, James, and John—apart from the Twelve and led them up to a high mountain. We are allowed, through the report of those disciples, a reverent glimpse of a sacred moment.

Mark wrote, probably from the account of Peter: "Jesus took with Him Peter, and James, and John, and led them up into an high mountain apart by themselves: and He was transfigured before them" (Mark 9:2).

Why should this momentous event in the life of Jesus, this thrilling experience in the life of His disciples, suffer neglect? Perhaps it is because we have no language which does verbal justice to it. We describe things by associating them with previous experience, and there is no human experience with which we can associate the Transfiguration. We understand some aspects of dying, and thus of the Crucifixion. We are aware of the agony of decision, and therefore have at least a faint idea of His suffering in Gethsemane. But a transfiguration we cannot fully understand—it is beyond our experience.

Splendor on the Mountaintop

The Transfiguration may have been a night scene. We are familiar with spotlights which illumine a performer on stage, but such lighting comes from outside the person. This kind of illumination was unusual because it came from within Jesus; "And His raiment became shining, exceeding white as snow," Mark tells us (9:3). The change in His face and clothing must have been an unforgettable sight. And again, it is so far removed from our experience we cannot imagine it clearly.

Perhaps Peter, James, and John later had less trouble than the others trying to picture in their minds a glorified Jesus at the Father's right hand. On the mountain they had beheld Him conversing with two other shining figures whom they somehow recognized as Moses and Elijah. It was a momentous, mysterious, majestic moment.

Why Moses and Elijah? Moses represented the Law; he was Israel's set-apart lawgiver, the one who received the Commandments from the hand of God. Elijah represented the prophets; he was a reformer, a spokesman for God to His erring people, a crusader for righteousness. He demanded that Israel remember the Law of God and obey it. Jesus was the link, for He testified, "Think not that I am come to destroy the Law, or the prophets: I am not come to destroy, but to fulfill" (Matt. 5:17). Christ was the completion of God's plan for mankind.

When the startled disciples beheld this incredible scene, they were speechless. Who could possibly speak the right words at such a moment? Who would know how to acknowledge the presence of men who had been gone from the earth for hundreds of years?

Perhaps it would have been better if the awed disciples had kept silent, if they had reverently worshiped the Lord in His newly-revealed glory. But Simon Peter—as usual—blurted out the first errant thought that came to his mind.

"Master," Peter stammered, "it is good for us to be here: and let us make three tabernacles; one for Thee, and one for Moses, and one for Elias" (Mark 9:5). In other words, his first thought was to hold onto the moment of glory, to cling to it, to preserve the experience indefinitely. "Why don't we stay right here?"

"He knew not what to say," Mark explained, "for they were very much afraid" (Mark 9:6, SCO).

Have you ever had a spiritual experience so tremendous that you didn't want it to end? You might never sense that particular joy again; you might never again know such an ecstatic moment or feel the presence of God in such power. That was Simon Peter's reaction. Peter was exhilarated and wanted to remain there on the mountaintop. But his request was foolish. Earth is never prepared to entertain heaven, and those who have been to heaven are never at home on earth anymore.

What about the needy people in the valley below? Peter didn't think of them. We, like Peter, are moved far more by our personal emotions than by the deep needs of a lost world. It would be so much easier, so much more pleasant to remain on the mountain peak, so much closer to heaven. It is difficult to return to the routine duties of the valley, to the sorrowing world of disillusionment, heartbreak, and sin. But Jesus didn't give His consent to construct those tabernacles. There was still work for Him and His disciples to do, just as there is still work for believers to accomplish in today's unbelieving world.

Perhaps the disciples were interested in conversing with Moses and Elijah because they understood them better than they did Jesus at that moment. Moses was a man of God accustomed to mountaintop experiences. God had called him to the top of awesome Mount Sinai and there had given him the Commandments for God's people. Then at the end of Moses' journey, God had shown him the Promised Land from the top of Mount Nebo. There God buried Moses—no one knows exactly where, we are informed.

Elijah had stood on Mount Carmel and confronted

the powerful priests of Baal. "Hear me, O Lord, hear me," he prayed, "that this people may know that Thou art the Lord God" (1 Kings 18:37). In answer, the heavens opened and fire fell. "If the Lord be God," Elijah entreated the people, "follow Him!" Years later, when God was ready for Elijah's ascent to heaven, He sent a fiery chariot to "shuttle" him.

It was not possible, however, for Jesus' disciples to commune with those two revered men of God. After Peter spoke up so impulsively, Moses and Elijah vanished. Only Jesus remained. There cannot be too much emphasis put on that: *Jesus only!* Neither Moses nor Elijah could be compared with Jesus.

Many recognize Jesus as a Master Teacher—but He is not only that. Some claim that He was a great humanitarian who pursued His cause, even to a martyr's death. But He was more than a man: He *was* and *is* the Son of God. He is the "great unlike." No one can be compared with Him, as the whole Book of Hebrews proclaims. Jesus only! If we know and fellowship with great servants of God, that is splendid. But the most important thing is to know Jesus and worship Him—Jesus only!

Preparation for the "Valley"

We can discover several purposes for this unique miracle known as the Transfiguration. First, it was designed to strengthen Jesus for the ordeal before Him, "a taste of rest to the weary traveler," as a great teacher once put it. The disciples overheard part of the conversation in which Moses and Elijah had been talking to Jesus about His "decease" or death at Jerusalem (see Luke 9:31).

Jesus was as much God as if He were never man, and as much man as if He were never God. In His humanity, He had come to a stupendous moment of choice. He could have ascended from this mountain of heavenly glory straight home to rejoin His Father—or He could descend the mountain and go forward to the Cross. He chose death on Golgotha's brow, to fulfill His role as the Lamb of God.

The Transfiguration strengthened Jesus for those difficult days ahead, for the kiss of Judas, the denials of Peter, the antagonism of the crowd, His nakedness on the cross. We hear in the background the faint prelude of Gethsemane: "Father, if there be any other way."

The Transfiguration was intended not only to strengthen Jesus for His sacrifice, but to bolster His disciples. He knew that in a little while they would be scattered and disillusioned. Christ was preparing them for trying days. As the disciples before us, we too need to draw from this vision of the glorified Christ strength to face the trying experiences of life—every frustrating day, every painful incident, every shadow of despair.

These three disciples would never again be the same. No man is ever the same after he sees Christ high and lifted up, as Isaiah saw God in the experience recorded in the sixth chapter of his prophetic book. The disciples described Jesus' clothes as "white as snow, so as no fuller [launderer] on earth can white [clean] them" (Mark 9:3). They beheld Him for the first time in His celestial body. His Transfiguration began from the inside and literally glowed outwardly until the very body itself seemed transformed. They received a taste of the glory of eternity in that moment. These three men, more than any others, must have gained an idea of what heaven is like.

When we glimpse the glory of the risen Christ, we want to be like Him. But we comprehend far too seldom the fact that a bit of the glory of eternity surrounds the Christian all the time—though we can't see it.

Recall the Old Testament account of how the servant of Elisha thought they were "done for." In dismay he exclaimed, "Alas, my master! What shall we do?"

"Fear not," Elisha reassured him, "for they that are with us are more than they that are with them" (2 Kings 6:16). Then Elisha prayed, "Lord...open his eyes, that he may see." The Bible says the young man then saw that "the mountain was full of horses and chariots of fire round about Elisha" (2 Kings 6:17).

Transfigured for Godliness

In one sense, the Transfiguration experience was only possible for Jesus. Yet His Transfiguration gives us a preview of our celestial bodies. Concerning this life also, God has a word to His discouraged children: "Be *ye* transformed!" We are to be transfigured in our lives here so others may see God in us.

What is the transformation Christ works in a person's life and how does it happen? God doesn't merely whitewash the outer life. The religious leaders of Jesus' day who attempted self-cleansing and boasted in self-righteousness, Jesus called "whitewashed sepulchres." Only God cleanses and renews the souls of mankind. When this change transpires in the inner man, his countenance, his walk, and his talk will not be the same. "Be ye transformed," the Apostle Paul wrote, "by the renewing of your mind, that ye may prove what is that good, and acceptable, and perfect, will of God" (Rom. 12:2).

When Moses came down from Mount Sinai after

talking with God, the Bible relates, "Moses wist [knew] not the skin of his face shone" (Ex. 34:29). He wasn't aware that he revealed what had happened to him, but the people saw it. If you have been with Jesus, people will be conscious of the difference He has made in you. "Let your light so shine before men," He taught, "that they may see your good works, and glorify your Father which is in heaven" (Matt. 5:16).

When Stephen, the first Christian martyr, was being stoned to death outside the gates of Jerusalem, He prayed in the same spirit as Jesus had prayed on the cross, "Lord, lay not this sin to their charge" (Acts 7:60). How could Stephen be so forgiving? Because, moments before, he had "looked up into heaven, and saw the glory of God, and Jesus standing on the right hand of God" (Acts 7:55). Earlier we are told, "All that sat in the council, looking steadfastly on him [Stephen], saw his face as it had been the face of an angel" (Acts 6:15). Why? Because Stephen had been transformed by God.

There can be no transformation of life until there has been a transformation of the prayer life. Jesus climbed the mountain to pray and was transfigured. When Moses talked with God, when Stephen saw the risen Christ standing to welcome him into heaven, their faces shone. When we pray, a transformation will be manifested in us.

There is no other means of capturing that inward radiance which was so evident to those who looked into the face of Jesus. That is why artists explain that the most difficult of all portraits to attempt is the face of Christ.

Transformation of spirit will produce transformation of life. The Apostle Paul wrote: "But we all, with open face beholding . . . the glory of the Lord, are changed into the same image from glory to glory, even as by the Spirit of the Lord" (2 Cor. 3:18).

There can be a mighty transformation in us if we are willing to present ourselves to God without reservation and let the Spirit perform His sanctifying work in us. We shall be changed from the image of the earthly to the image of the heavenly. In this restless day, when the world seeks a God it has not met, may we show forth Jesus' glory that He may be seen in us.

9 His Selfless Sufferings

Luke 22:44

Two gardens mentioned in the Bible are important to a person's salvation. The first is the Garden of Eden, where paradise was created and lost. The other is the Garden of Gethsemane. These two gardens were arenas of destiny—sites of world crises. The world's most staggering silent battle occurred in Gethsemane. All the forces of evil converged against Christ there.

After Jesus had observed the Passover supper with His disciples in Jerusalem, He had many precious truths to share with them. The hours wore on. Late that night, those who remained walked with Him east across the Kidron Valley to rest in the tranquil spot called the Garden of Gethsemane, a little grove of trees on the slopes of the Mount of Olives.

Today that spot is a tourist attraction. Every day of the year people mill around on the side of that hill. They reach out to the ancient trees, hoping the guard or the guide will turn away so they can snatch a souvenir. When they come back home they exclaim, "Yes, I've been to Gethsemane."

I've been there too—and yet I haven't. Geographically we can visit the place, but I doubt if any of us have shared anything of the sorrow, suffering, and agony that Jesus, the Son of God, underwent that night. I doubt if we can ever claim that we have actually been to Gethsemane with Him.

"I come to the Garden alone," we sing, "while the dew is still on the roses." But do we mean that? Throughout the dark hours of Jesus' anguish, do not our eyes grow heavy with sleep like those who were supposed to watch outside the gate? Eight of them were there and three were inside with the Master, about the distance of "a stone's cast."

As we approach Gethsemane, we should heed the admonition God gave Moses at the burning bush: "Put off thy shoes from off thy feet, for the place whereon thou stand is holy ground" (Ex. 3:5). In Gethsemane, we enter into the holy of holies in the life of Jesus.

Only a priceless few times has God pulled back the curtain to reveal the depths of Jesus' soul as He does here. In Old Testament days, when the priest entered the tabernacle and in later times the temple, he first offered a sacrifice for the sins of the people in the outer court. Then he went beyond the veil, into the sacred holy of holies to present the blood of the sacrifice at the mercy seat. Anyone other than the high priest entering that awesome place would have been struck dead. Only after Christ's crucifixion was the veil of the temple torn open so that everyone was able to peer into that hallowed room which was considered the abode of God on earth.

The Dark Night of the Soul

In the Gospels, the disciples—especially John in chapter 17—described what occurred in Gethsemane. "How could they?" you may ask. "Weren't they asleep?"

They slept fitfully, perhaps. Certainly they could not have been completely unmindful of Jesus' sorrow. They were supposed to be His friends; surely they felt part of His heaviness of heart. Or maybe there came a time during His post-resurrection ministry when Jesus sat down and shared with them what had happened that night in Gethsemane. He may have opened to them His heart as He did that day on the Emmaus road when He walked with two disciples and opened to them the Scriptures concerning Himself.

Imagine how His "inner circle" must have felt when they heard Him say dejectedly, "Sleep on now, and take your rest! The time has passed. I don't need you as much as I did."

Their severest mistake was in thinking that this night was for sleeping. They did not have spiritual perception. They did not have enough insight to recognize His sorrow, so they slept, blindly thinking this night would be much like all other nights.

Yet that night the Garden of Gethsemane witnessed the bitterest anguish of the Master—possibly even more bitter than the Cross. For it was here that the battle of the Cross was won. The solitude of His soul was an exceeding heaviness to the Man of Sorrows. It was a strange solitariness, an unusual loneliness. There are various solitudes, some by space and others by spirit. Jesus and His disciples were about twenty paces apart, and yet eternity separated them.

The sun views enough of the sorrows and tragedies of the world, but the moon sees more than the sun. For there is more sin and sorrow, more violence and wickedness in the darkness. The evil of this world flourishes under the cover of night. The moon looked down that night on the holiest and sorest sorrow that ever came into any man's life.

Paul's beloved physician-friend, Luke, wrote a vivid description, though he was not there: "And being in an agony He prayed more earnestly; and His sweat was, as it were, great drops of blood falling down to the ground" (Luke 22:44). The words "and being in an agony" fit most of our life stories. Every man descends to some night of nights and realizes what it means to be in agony. The experience is what St. John of the Cross called "the dark night of the soul." For Jesus it wasn't the burden of one lost sheep, the straying of one boy, one erring father, or one backslidden loved one—it was the combined sorrows of the entire world that weighed Him down with loneliness and agony.

Because of His intense suffering for us, our suffering becomes more bearable. Every person may find in this circumstance a kinship with Jesus. There in the wilderness when He was tempted, and here in the Garden, we experience a feeling of fellowship with Him that we never find elsewhere, for we are partners in sorrow and agony.

Abandoned by Man and God

On the part of those disciples Jesus loved and defended, there seemed to be an unbelievable lack of concern. Their insensitivity, cowardice, and lethargy surely pierced Him as arrows. Judas kissed him. Simon Peter cursed and denied Him. Thomas doubted Him. At this moment of crisis, Jesus pleaded, "My heart is nearly breaking . . . stay here and keep watch with Me" (Matt. 26:38, PH).

They failed Him, and they could easily have tried to alibi with the excuse, "Lord, all we are doing is sleeping!" But is anything worse than sleeping when

God needs us? Is anything worse than indifference when it is time for revival? Is anything worse than not standing up to be counted in a moral crisis? We can never fully enter into the sorrow of the Lord's moment of despair in Gethsemane and the suffering He endured—but we should try!

"My God, My God, why hast Thou forsaken Me?" Jesus cried out from the cross. We look back on the Cross with rejoicing that His death saves us, but His Cross also shatters. We will have both experiences in our lives. The "cross" that came into the life of Abraham shattered him—could he slay his promised son at God's command? The "cross" that came into the life of Job shattered him—his wife advised, "Curse God and die!"

The Cross that came into the life of Christ shattered Him—the holy, sinless One "became sin for us." "If He be the King of Israel," sneered the religious leaders of the nation, "let Him now come down from the cross, and we will believe Him" (Matt. 27:42). "If Thou be the Christ," railed one of the desperate, dying thieves, "save Thyself and us!" (Luke 23:39) The Cross saved us, but for our sakes, Jesus could not save Himself.

Willing to Pay the Cost

The Cross was the result of Christ's decision in the Garden. If Jesus had not agreed, "Father, Thy will, not Mine, be done," there would be no remedy for the agony we all suffer in this life or would suffer in the life to come because of sin. In the Garden, He was offered a cup of bitterness which became our cup of blessing. We vow that God answers prayer. Did His Son's prayer go unnoticed by God? It seems like that to some people.

Jesus looked at the cup and recoiled from it, the

Bible reveals. This was a natural reaction of His flesh. This earthly tabernacle in which we live is not self—soul is self. You may wear a new suit that makes you draw back from grease that might soil it. There is an instinctive withdrawal of the body from agents that might injure it. Jesus came down from heaven and wore the flesh of mankind for a specific reason and for a limited season.

What was in this cup? Jesus, the sinless One, looked in it and saw all the horror the Cross would hold for His holy nature. He is the only One who has ever been able to truly lament, "Behold, and see if there be any sorrow like unto my sorrow" (Lam. 1:12). We may have felt like that, but we can't mean it in the same measure Jesus meant it.

"Father, if it be possible, let it pass from Me!" He cried out. Why? What was in the cup? Surely it was the distilled accumulation of Adamic sin. Everything: past, present, and future—my sins, your sins, all of them together, mingled in that disgusting, revolting cup. All our poisonous hate and vindictiveness. All the pain of suffering, loneliness, and sorrow. Jesus became sin for us, and when He did, God could no longer look on His Son, because He could not look on sin. Jesus became sin in our place.

The agony of Jesus' suffering was almost unbearable, perhaps all the more so because it was spiritual and not merely physical, like the pain of the cross itself. Already His disciples had begun to account Him and His cause a failure. One of them had sold Him out, and the others would soon desert or deny Him. Didn't God care anymore? Had God no concern about His Son? I doubt if there has ever been a cry of sorrow on earth as deep, as all-inclusive as the one Jesus uttered in Gethsemane.

His cup of sorrow ultimately became our cup of

salvation. His agony was climaxed with the glorious submission of the Son to the will of His Father. "If there be any other way," He prayed. At first there was revulsion, but Jesus actually was willing: "If not . . . Thy will be done!"

Whoever counts on another scheme of salvation except the Cross is lost, doomed, damned. There is no other way! If God had let Jesus go to the cross when there was another way, He would have been guilty of heinous cruelty. God allowed His own Son to be nailed to the cross because there was no other means of saving us. The way of morality, the way of human goodness, the way of material goods offered—these would not and will not make it.

"I am the way, the truth, and the life," Jesus claimed. "No man comes unto the Father, but by Me" (John 14:6). What we call the Lord's Prayer—"Our Father, which art in heaven"—is the pattern for prayer that Jesus gave His disciples. It is often called "The Model Prayer." Here is the Lord's own, His deepest prayer: "Nevertheless, not My will but Thine be done!"

In Eden, Adam and Eve declared in effect, "Not Thy will be done, God, but mine!" In Gethsemane, the Son was speaking in reverse: "Not My will be done, but Thine." This is our Lord's prayer; this is the prayer we must utter on our faces before God: "Not my will, but *Thine* be done!"

Jesus was fully conscious of what His prayer meant: the bitter cup of the Cross. We must confess that we can't imagine His total purity or holiness; we can't experience sorrow or pray as He did. Though we may pray, "Lord, I want cleansing, whatever the cost," we sometimes don't realize the price of what we are asking.

But when Jesus prayed, "Father, Thy will be done,"

He knew what it would cost Him. In the crucible of Gethsemane, His love and the Father's love were welded together to forge our salvation.

10 His Atoning Cross

Hebrews 2:9

"Familiarity breeds contempt," goes the old expression. Does it? Is it possible that we have become too familiar with the story of the Cross? If we could hear it anew, as if for the first time, perhaps we could regain a sense of the awe and majesty of God's love. The old rugged cross should be, not in the back of our minds, but in the front of our hearts.

Unfortunately, the contrary is often true. Concerning the story of Calvary we often develop a mental block. The miracle of Jesus' feeding 5,000 people with five loaves of bread and two little fish captures our imagination. He was able to make the blind see and the lame walk and the dead breathe again. These miracles make us rejoice. The glory of the Transfiguration lifts our hearts. But when we come to His crucifixion, we shake our heads.

How can we face the reality of the Cross? It is death, and it is ugly. The Roman Empire, which used the cross as its chief form of capital punishment, admitted it was vile and brutal. No Roman citizen, regardless of his crime, had to suffer its ignominy.

The cross was reserved for slaves, foreigners, and incorrigible criminals. Always done in public, crucifixion was designed to insure good behavior in those who saw it for a long time afterward. It put the fear of Rome into the people's hearts.

It seems strange that He who had created the earth died as a foreigner on it. Truly, Jesus had no home. "The birds of the air have nests," He said, "but the Son of man hath not where to lay His head" (Matt. 8:20). He had no decent place to be born, only an unused manger. He had no place to die—only a criminal's cross. His own people screamed, "He is an alien. He is not one of us. Crucify Him!"

We do not even like to talk about Gethsemane. The name of that garden means more than simply a locality; it is a word implying agony and we shrink from it. It is necessary, however, for us to face the Cross, for it is the focal point of the Gospel. "But we see Jesus," observed the writer to the Hebrews, "who was made a little lower than the angels . . . that He by the grace of God should taste death for every man" (Heb. 2:9).

Charles Haddon Spurgeon, one of the greatest preachers who ever lived, was accused to his face that his sermons were all exactly alike. "You are right," Spurgeon admitted. "I take a text and make a beeline for the Cross every time I preach." Unless we magnify the atoning death of Jesus on the cross, we are not preaching the Gospel of Christ, regardless of whatever else we might preach.

Christ was not the first man to be crucified, nor was He the first man to die for the cause of righteousness. But He was the first and only man ever to die *in our place*. At Golgotha, God was at His best and man was at his worst! What they did to Jesus should sicken us! But the physical agony He sustained was not His only suffering; the shame of the cross was undoubtedly the most humiliating indignity that Jesus suffered.

At Calvary

Most of the religions of the world are religions for men—women have no place. The only religion that has a central place for women is Christianity. Men were scarce when Jesus died, like they are scarce today when we wish they would stand with us. Women stood around His cross, shameful sight though it was. The hardened soldiers stripped all clothing from the suspended bodies. Criminals were shamed and humiliated in their exposure before the world.

No wonder these soldiers expected to be cursed! They looked at Jesus in surprise when He had no harsh words for them. The centurion shook his head and proclaimed, "Surely this was the Son of God!"

According to secular history, the soldiers who drew this "detail of death" used cheap wine made of hyssop to deaden their own nerves, to fortify themselves when they struck the nails, saw the spurting blood, and heard the cries of those they crucified.

It seems incredible that Jesus accepted all this voluntarily. "I lay down My life . . ." He affirmed, "no man takes it from Me" (John 10:17-18). Also, He said, "Greater love hath no man than this, that a man lay down his life for his friends" (John 15:13). I wonder if He thought He had a friend in that group. It seemed that His enemies were all there.

God did not force Jesus out of heaven, push Him into the world, and make Him go to the Cross. But from the time of Adam's sin, God warned the serpent that Eve's seed should bruise his head, though "thou shalt bruise His heel" (Gen. 3:15).

The whole scheming, scorning, sinful world

thought this was the end of Jesus and all His work. Apparently no man was ever so ingloriously defeated, so ignominiously crushed, so completely dead. He was nailed to a tree—helpless, shamed, and in terrible pain.

But that was not the whole story. At the gates of heaven, twelve legions of angels strained to come to Jesus' rescue—172,000 of them waited for His command, but Jesus did not utter the word. Voluntarily He bore the burden of sin that caused His holy Father to turn away.

Jesus explained to His disciples beforehand that He would be rejected and humiliated. "For He shall be delivered unto the Gentiles, and shall be mocked, and spitefully entreated, and spitted on: and they shall scourge Him, and put Him to death: and the third day He shall rise again" (Luke 18:32-33).

The betrayal by Judas Iscariot, the denial by Simon Peter, the horrendous death on the cross—all this was endured by the world's most sensitive Man. After His arrest, His disciples concluded that His was a lost cause; now it was "every man for himself" and they fled in terror. Only the women remained.

People today are shocked when unruly crowds spit at an ambassador. But mocking onlookers spat on Jesus. Imagine, people spitting in the face of God and God not striking them dead! How much the Son of God suffered at our hands! Many taunted Him, "If Thou be the Son of God, come down [from the cross]!"

It wasn't the first time that men of God have been challenged to leave what God asked them to do. Nehemiah was building the walls of Jerusalem when critics and enemies called, "Nehemiah, come down and parley with us." "I am doing a great work, and I cannot come down," Nehemiah retorted firmly (see

Neh. 6:1-4).

"Come down and prove to us that You are the Son of God!" the skeptics called to Jesus. But He had no need to prove anything. He *was* the Son of God. When you are something, you don't have to prove it. It is when you aren't sure of yourself that you try to offer proof.

"Come down from the cross," the crowd taunted Him. The Son of God, Redeemer of heaven and earth, could have given the same answer as Nehemiah: "I am doing a great work and I *cannot* come down."

Thomas Carlyle, a famous English agnostic, hesitated in front of a show window in Paris as he looked at a crucifix. He commented—half to himself, but loud enough for his companions to hear him—"Little man, you have had your day!" That's what he thought about Jesus. The priests, the scribes, the soldiers, and Pilate thought, "Little man, you have had your day."

Jesus had commanded the winds and waves and multiplied the loaves and fishes, but He had had His day, His enemies thought.

No, He hadn't *had* His day. He was *having* His day! He was doing what He had come to do. He was making atonement for sin. He will yet have His day; for there's a great day coming! He shall return in all of His glory as judge and ruler of the earth. Then wicked men won't sneer at Him. They will cry to the rocks and the hills to fall on them and hide them from His sight.

A Ransom for Many

Christ's return will be a blessed event, as was His first advent, but the most blessed event in all history was His atonement. Jesus defined His ministry, "The Son of man came not to be ministered unto, but to minister, and to give His life a ransom for many"

(Matt. 20:28).

The word *atonement*, which we hear often and seldom fully understand, means "to cover." His was a vicarious, substitutionary death in that He died for our sin, not His own. The basic concept is to reconcile those who have been separated, making possible a reunion. Christ removed sin, which had built a barrier between us and God, thus reuniting us with our Father.

Vicarious means to act as a substitute for another. It refers back to the doctrine of the scapegoat taught in the Old Testament, where the high priest symbolically put on the scapegoat the sins of the people and sent it into the wilderness. The Bible talks about the scapegoat "taking away" sins.

Isaiah does not talk about an animal, but about a man, the God-Man: "All we like sheep have gone astray; we have turned every one to his own way, and the Lord hath laid on Him [Jesus] the iniquity of us all" (Isa. 53:6).

When people were praising John the Baptist, he protested: "I indeed baptize you with water unto repentance: but He that comes after me is mightier than I . . . He shall baptize you with the Holy Ghost, and with fire" (Matt. 3:11). "Behold the Lamb of God," John declared, pointing Jesus out to his disciples, "which takes away the sin of the world" (John 1:29). For "without shedding of blood there is no remission [of sin]" (Heb. 9:22).

Jesus was the only One who ever had a life to give away. We can't die for ourselves because we don't own ourselves. We are the slaves of sin. You can't sell or give away a piece of mortgaged property because you don't own it outright; at least part of it belongs to another. We are mortgaged property, if you please. Sin has left its stain on us and we are worthless. The stench of death is already on us, and we are fit for nothing but the junk heap.

When Christ the Son of God died, it seemed to those who followed Him that all hope was gone. The sun had set and it was dark forever.

But morning was coming! The suffering of Christ led to victory! "God hath raised Him up, having loosed the pains of death: because it was not possible that He should be holden of it," Luke wrote (Acts 2:24). When He cried on the cross, "It is finished!" those words did not mean what they seemed to mean. It wasn't possible that any grave in this whole world could hold Him. His seeming defeat turned into victory.

Sin and evil had done their worst and left their mark, for He will always bear the nail prints in His hands. Even today, sin has made its inroads on the church. Scoffers try to say the church is worthless and might as well be scrapped. But it is not as weak as it seems. God still lives. God still is on His throne and He still keeps His promises. God isn't dead and God hasn't had His day. His Great Day is yet to come.

Victory in Jesus

In a past century, when long-distance communication was nothing more than flag signals, a heated battle was being fought in France. Before darkness closed in over the English Channel, flags on the French shoreline spelled out, "Wellington defeated. . . ." All night long that terrible news spread across England. It seemed that the cause of liberty was doomed. But when morning came, the signalman repeated the message and was able to complete it: "Wellington defeated the enemy!" What rejoicing followed that night of sorrow!

We are awaiting God's daybreak for His message to

be completed. It seems now that the night is dark and weeping is constant. But one day hence Jesus is returning in victory. "Weeping may endure for a night," wrote the psalmist, "but joy comes in the morning" (Ps. 30:5).

We must never leave Jesus hanging on the cross, as many do. There was triumph on that tree! On Golgotha, God won the victory. Jesus Christ's suffering was voluntary and it was vicarious. But more than anything else, it was victorious! Our Lord won the war and conquered sin for all eternity, as evidenced by His resurrection from the grave.

> *Christ the Lord is ris'n today,*
> *Alleluia!*
> *Sons of men and angels say,*
> *Alleluia!*
>
> *Raise your joys and triumphs high,*
> *Alleluia!*
> *Sing ye heav'ns and earth reply,*
> *Alleluia!*
>
> —Charles Wesley

11 His Authoritative Voice

Isaiah 42:16

What does serving a risen, ascended, victorious Christ involve? According to Isaiah, God promised, "I will make darkness light before them, and crooked things straight. These things will I do unto them, and not forsake them" (Isa. 42:16).

Does God still have the power today He did in Bible times? Can He still work mighty miracles? Is He still able to remake communities, challenge churches, and revitalize our spiritual lives?

Many crises occur in life—personal, economic, natural. Because the world around us changes, and we change, we often wonder if God changes too. Is it possible for us to live in confidence that the victory is the Lord's? Can we feel certain that faith and hope will prevail? Do we listen for the voice of God and know assuredly that He is the One who is able to meet all difficulties?

Authority over Death

When Jesus was going to the cross, soldiers guarded Him. It is likely that many spectators were not sure who He was. They only noticed another man going to his death, because this trail to Golgotha was used repeatedly by the Roman soldiers. Some who sympathized followed at a distance; those who loved Jesus wept in travail.

"Weep not for Me," the Master advised them, "but weep for yourselves, and for your children" (Luke 23:28). The Saviour, even as He dragged His cross, never lost faith in God's victory. He had the assurance that He was in the will of God. "He shall not cry, nor lift up, nor cause His voice to be heard in the street," declared Isaiah (Isa. 42:2). His death was not an accident; the enmity of the whole world could not kill Him unless His Father willed it. His death was not waste, but victory! The world cannot fathom the paradox of the Cross.

The soldiers returned to break the legs of those who had been crucified, to hasten their death; they came to Jesus, and said, "He is dead already." It was as though they had said, "He is finished!" But they had not been listening closely: earlier He had called out, "*It* is finished!"

"*It*"—the redemptive work that Christ came to do—was finished! His words were not a whimper, or an apology, but a victorious shout. It was a song of the Saviour, for He turned His face toward heaven after the darkness and lifted up His voice, "Father, into Thy hands I commend My spirit." He had accomplished His mission.

Because the grave did not and could not finish Him, mankind has had to reevaluate history. When someone asked Talleyrand, famous prime minister under Louis XIV of France, how he could drum up a following to start a new religion, he answered, "There is one plan which you might at least try. I should recommend that you get yourself crucified and rise again the third day."

Jesus did precisely that. Because He was victorious over the grave, His enemies concocted lies to conceal the fact. The priests claimed that someone had come and stolen His body away. Down through the centuries, rather than admit what they declared impossible, others have claimed that He was not really dead. But this was the only grave that was not victorious over the body placed in it.

When Napoleon was winning victory after victory across Europe, his voice and presence gave zeal and spirit to his troops; "Your emperor is with you!" was sufficient for them. But when he was defeated at Waterloo, he was no longer able to inspire his troops. Alexander the Great conquered the known world with his massive army, but after he died, that army disintegrated.

Charlemagne met death in battle—and he was no longer a victor. He demanded, as his last request, that he be buried upright because he wanted to be in a position of command, not of helplessness. Years later, when the grave was opened, on the scroll that had slipped from his hands were the words, "What shall it profit a man, if he shall gain the whole world, and lose his own soul?" (Mark 8:36)

If you want to gain the world, Jesus taught, you must lose yourself. He came into the world, born of a humble maiden, cradled in a manger. He walked the paths of Palestine all the way to the Cross in order that He might lose Himself in the lives of His people. He never owned real estate. He was poverty-stricken by today's standards. He was condemned, despised, and rejected. How then was this Man triumphant?

In the first place, He could truthfully attest, "The Father that sent Me bears witness of Me" (John 8:18). Regardless of the world's opinion, God's applause is more important than all else.

"The Father and I are one," Jesus claimed. "I am in the Father, and the Father in Me" (John 14:10). When a disciple asked, "Lord, show us the Father," the Master chided, "Have I been so long time with you, and yet hast thou not known Me, Philip? He that hath seen Me hath seen the Father" (John 14:9). The Father testified more than once to His identification with Jesus Christ. At the beginning of the Lord's earthly ministry, Jesus walked down into the baptismal waters of the Jordan. As He came out, a dove came down from the opened heavens and a voice spoke from above, saying, "This is My beloved Son, in whom I am well pleased" (Matt. 3:17). There was no doubt in the minds of those who stood by the River Jordan. These were not the words of John the Baptist. This was a voice from higher up.

Most of the religious leaders of the Jews differed with God in their opinion of Jesus and His claims. "He hath spoken blasphemy!" declared the high priest. "What further need have we of witnesses? Behold, now ye have heard His blasphemy" (Matt. 26:65).

Was Jesus a successful Man in spite of their opinion? Teachers admit that Jesus was in truth a Master Teacher. Men dedicated to medicine note that Jesus' healing touch was beyond that of any man; He was truly the Great Physician. Any sane king that ever walked the earth would call Him a compassionate and selfless leader. And the day will come when all will cast their crowns at His feet, saying, "Thou art the King of kings and Lord of lords."

Crown Him with many crowns,
the Lamb upon His throne;
Hark! how the heav'nly anthem drowns

all music but its own!
Awake, my soul, and sing
of Him who died for thee,
And hail Him as thy matchless King
thro' all eternity.

Crown Him the Lord of life,
who triumphed o'er the grave,
And rose victorious in the strife
for those He came to save;
His glories now we sing,
who died, and rose on high,
Who died eternal life to bring,
and lives that death may die.

Crown Him the Lord of love;
behold His hands and side,
Rich wounds, yet visible above,
in beauty glorified;
All hail, Redeemer, hail!
for Thou hast died for me;
Thy praise and glory shall not fail
thro'out eternity.

—Matthew Bridges

The Voice of Men

Jesus was vastly interested in what people said about Him. He turned to His disciples on one occasion and asked, "Whom do men say that I the Son of man am?"

His disciples answered, "John the Baptist: but some say, Elias; and others, one of the prophets."

"But whom do ye say that I am?" Jesus persisted.

Simon Peter, voicing what he felt in his heart—the hope and faith of the years he had walked with the Master—replied, "Thou art the Christ, the Son of the living God" (Matt. 16:16).

There is no place to hide from the Son of God; He is inescapable. "Before Abraham was, I am," He declared (John 8:58). He is still asking men today, "Whom do you say that I am?" Your whole life witnesses to the world your belief in God or lack of it.

At the foot of the cross, some of the spectators acted as though Jesus were eternally dead. Some live today as if Jesus did not rise from the dead and God will never demand judgment. But the voice of the Victor one day will claim this world as His own, and the judgment of God will fall on all who have rejected Him.

He who will one day be the righteous Judge of all the earth stood silently before Pilate, the Roman governor, to find out what the courts of the world thought about Him. Pilate hesitated. From the secular point of view, there was no reason why the cynical Roman should suddenly have developed a conscience—except that for the first time he realized that he was in the presence of a Man who was completely innocent.

Some of us might not be guilty of crimes with which we are charged, but all of us recognize we are guilty, somewhere, sometime. In the sight of all men, Jesus' character was flawless, as befitting the Son of God He claimed to be. No fault was found in Him.

Pilate, because of his wife's insistence, because of his probing conscience, turned to the multitude and confessed, "I find no fault in this Man." This was the only time in all history that any duly appointed officer had said, "I believe the man who stands before me is absolutely and completely faultless."

The Living and Written Word

More than the opinions of the courts and more than the thoughts of men, we want to know what the record of God says. For didn't Jesus claim to be the long-awaited Messiah, the Saviour of mankind?

What does God's Word say about Him? The Apostle John started his account of the Lord's life with the statement that "the Word was made flesh and dwelt among us" (John 1:14). He is the everlasting Christ, the Word of God. "There is none other name under heaven given among men, whereby we must be saved," Peter declared to the Sanhedrin with surprising boldness (Acts 4:12).

Jesus' ministry was one of teaching, healing, preaching. When He approached the end of His ministry and the Cross loomed immediately in front of Him, the mighty voice from heaven came again on the Mount of Transfiguration. His three astonished disciples were commanded, "This is My beloved Son; hear Him" (Mark 9:7). Yes, hear Jesus, for He is the only One who can mend hearts and change lives.

What do we hear from the voice of the Victor? "Come unto Me," Jesus besought those who doubted and were discouraged, "all ye that labor and are heavy laden, and I will give you rest" (Matt. 11:28). Through Jesus, God is hearable.

"Heaven and earth shall pass away," Jesus declared, "but My words shall not pass away" (Matt. 24:35). God is durable. We live in a changing, turbulent society, but God remains unchanging. Jesus Christ is "the same yesterday, and today, and forever" (Heb. 13:8). God gave us, not a monument, but a Man—the Son of man who is also the Son of God. Everything else but His kingdom shall pass away.

Hear what Jesus has to say concerning the devil: "Thou shalt not tempt the Lord thy God. . . . Get thee hence, Satan" (Matt. 4:7, 10). Shortly before the Cross, Jesus said to Peter, "Satan hath desired to have you, that he may sift you as wheat" (Luke 22:31). But as the Apostle Paul wrote, "There hath no temptation taken you but such as is common to man; but God is faithful, who . . . will with the temptation also make a way to escape" (1 Cor. 10:13).

Then what does the voice of the Victor say to those who are defeated? The Apostle Paul wrote under the inspiration of the Holy Spirit, "And we know that all things work together for good to them that love God" (Rom. 8:28). Then Paul added, "Who shall separate us from the love of Christ? Shall tribulation, or distress, or persecution, or famine, or nakedness, or peril, or sword? . . . Nay, in all these things we are more than conquerors through Him that loved us" (Rom. 8:35, 37). This is no uncertain voice; this echoes the authoritative voice of God, who has the power of this world in His hands.

"But what does He have to say about death?" you may ask. Jesus didn't say much about death. Rather than talking about it, He conquered it! Therefore Paul could pen this veritable hymn of praise, "When this corruptible shall have put on incorruption, and this mortal shall have put on immortality, then shall be brought to pass the saying that is written, 'Death is swallowed up in victory.' . . . Thanks be to God, which gives us the victory through our Lord Jesus Christ" (1 Cor. 15:54, 57).

Jesus conquered death and one day, through Him, we shall also be victorious over the grave. As long as we live in this physical body, death will threaten us, but the voice of Jesus triumphantly declares that He overcame death forever. "For as in Adam all die, even so in Christ shall all be made alive" (1 Cor. 15:22). The body will be laid aside, but the spirit will return to God who gave it, there to await the resurrection of the body.

"I am the resurrection, and the life." Jesus spoke

those consoling words to Mary and Martha at the grave of Lazarus. "He that believes in Me, though he were dead, yet shall he live. And whosoever lives and believes in Me shall never die. Believe thou this?" (John 11:25-26) This is the voice of the Victor!

Death may crush lives and break hearts; it may seem the apparent victor, but it shall not eternally triumph. One day God will take away death's sting, open the graves, and reunite loved ones, abolishing death forever. "O death, where is thy sting? O grave, where is thy victory?" (1 Cor. 15:55)

"The Lord Himself shall descend from heaven with a shout," Paul also wrote, "with the voice of the archangel, and with the trump of God: and the dead in Christ shall rise first" (1 Thes. 4:16). This will be the voice of the Victor!

Heeding His Call

Is your heart asleep to the things of Christ, or is He real to you today? God is speaking to you, "This is Jesus, My beloved Son. Hear Him!"

When we listen to Jesus, we hear this blessed invitation: "Behold, I stand at the door, and knock: if any man hear My voice, and open the door, I will come in to him, and will sup with him, and he with Me" (Rev. 3:20).

12 His Holy Name

Philippians 2:9

"What's in a name?" This question has been immortalized by poets. It frequently has engaged the attention of philosophers. The Bible too places considerable emphasis on names and their meanings. A parenthetical phrase in Numbers 32:38 notices, "their names being changed." It was possible then, and it is possible now, for a name to be changed. But it is a solemn matter and cannot be done without due process of law.

In some cultures, names have been considered extremely important. They were distinctive, descriptive, and had deep personal meaning. Parents often waited until their child showed some progress or had some adventure in life before they gave him a name that implied that particular character trait.

We live in an impersonal age. In the past, banks hired experienced bookkeepers who gave check signatures careful scrutiny to see if they were authentic before certifying them. Now checks are put into a sorting machine, and the numbers printed on them determine distribution into the proper accounts.

Each of us has so many numbers that we sometimes merely seem to be another point of reference in an age that is totally computerized.

The name of Jesus Christ will never become just a number. His is the greatest name in human history. It has remained unaltered from before the beginning of time. How can we describe what that name means to us? We can't begin to measure it; we can find no meaningful number to attach to Him. Our minds are not able to encompass the true magnitude of the Son of God.

The Name of Heaven

About 800 years before the Messiah appeared, Isaiah attempted to depict this indescribable individual: "For unto us a child is born, unto us a son is given: and the government shall be upon His shoulder; and His name shall be called Wonderful, Counselor, The mighty God, The everlasting Father, The Prince of Peace" (Isa. 9:6).

Before a portrait of Christ we may stand appreciatively, seeing through the eyes of the artist a few attributes he imagined in that Face. Yet we can't help feeling that the portrait is imperfect. It does not adequately portray the face of Jesus—no portrait can. The same is true of His hands—the hands that were nailed to the cross yet broke bread three days later at a table in Emmaus. It was by His hands that the disciples recognized Him. Who can describe His hands? What was it like to feel their gentle touch in blessing, in healing, in friendship?

"On human lips, the name of Jesus is the sweetest name in any language," T. DeWitt Talmadge has said. "It is easier," he affirmed, "for a child to be taught that name than the word *Mother*. It comes easily to the tongue. It is not a harsh name, but a name of beauty and sweetness."

When Gipsy Smith, an evangelist of a former generation, held a revival meeting in the Will Rogers Coliseum in Fort Worth, I was at an impressionable age. It was the largest religious gathering I had ever seen. Each night after the invitation had been given, Gipsy would close the service by singing in his unusually mellow voice, "Wonderful, wonderful Jesus! In the heart He implanteth a song." He sent us away with the name of Jesus in our hearts. We could not help but feel that it was wondrous to speak the name of Jesus.

Charles Wesley wrote about the name of Jesus in the hymn, "O For a Thousand Tongues to Sing," which has been a favorite for generations. The third verse reads:

> *Jesus—the Name that charms our fears,*
> *That bids our sorrows cease;*
> *'Tis music in the sinner's ears,*
> *'Tis life, and health, and peace.*

The Name of Honor

When Jesus taught His disciples to pray, He tried to instill in them a sense of reverence for God. They were to pray, "Hallowed be Thy name." We are not to profane the name of God or that of His Son, Jesus Christ. We are not to handle the name of Jesus as though it were commonplace or unimportant. Respect for the name of Jesus Christ must be reclaimed today, beginning with those who call themselves Christians. God is omnipresent; His Spirit is with us and within us and dwells in believers over the whole earth.

There is a vast difference between familiarity with God and informality in worship. When we bow our heads in the house of God, when we call on the name of Jesus Christ, there must be that awesome reverence which is due the great God of the universe. That respect should extend to His Son and to His Word. God is not "the Man Upstairs" proclaimed by a Gospel song of years ago. He is not a back-slapping clown, a heavenly St. Nick. He is God, blessed forever.

God's Son and His Word have been the particular point of attack by atheists and infidels. When Thomas Paine came to America over a century and a half ago, he boasted as he left his ship, "When I get through, there will not be five Bibles left in America." He thought that he could spread his "Age of Reason" philosophy and cause people to abandon the Word of God. But the Bible is still a bestseller, and the name of Thomas Paine is almost forgotten. Young people today usually ask, "Thomas who?"

The name of Jesus Christ has never been popular with everyone, it is true. Only one of the ten lepers He healed came back to fall down before Him. But there will always be those who care, those who follow Him. Through these, His name and His message continue to have an impact on the entire world.

It is incredible that any person who comprehends in any measure the holiness of God and the love of Jesus Christ should drag the name of Jesus down into the gutter.

"God also hath highly exalted Him," the Apostle Paul wrote, "and given Him a name which is above every name" (Phil. 2:9). Together, the names of *Jesus* and *Christ* stand for the person and work of the Godhead in human affairs. The name *Christ* indicates His positon as God's anointed, His claim to lordship over the earth. *Christ* in Greek is the same word as *Messiah* in Hebrew. For centuries the Jews had been looking for their Messiah, eagerly awaiting the time when God's Deliverer would come and save them from their enemies and rule over them in righteousness and peace.

The Greek name *Jesus* (*Joshua* in Hebrew) means "Saviour." The angel informed Joseph, "Thou shalt call His name Jesus, for He shall save His people from their sins" (Matt. 1:21). *Jesus* became His name of deep humiliation, His personal name as a man among men, suffering and dying for them.

"Isn't this the son of Mary?" asked some of the people of His hometown. "Isn't this the carpenter's son?" Yes, He was the Son of Mary, the foster son of the carpenter, Joseph, who lived in Nazareth. The people knew Him only as Jesus—His personal name—not as the Son of God, the Messiah, the Christ.

"I am the Good Shepherd," Jesus preached, "and know My own sheep, and they know Me, just as My Father knows Me and I know the Father; and I lay down My life for the sheep" (John 10:14-15, TLB).

He was "the Lamb slain from the foundation of the world" (Rev. 13:8). The accounts of His trial and crucifixion illustrate the prophecies of Isaiah 53.

"No one can kill Me without My consent," He said. "I lay down My life voluntarily" (John 10:18, TLB).

When we come to Calvary, our hearts should overflow with the warm glow of loving gratitude. When we realize that His sacrifice there was substitutionary, that He accepted our place of death, we cannot help but love Him.

See, from His head, His hands, His feet,
Sorrow and love flow mingled down;
Did e'er such love and sorrow meet,
Or thorns compose so rich a crown?

Were the whole realm of nature mine

That were a present far too small;
Love so amazing, so divine,
Demands my soul, my life, my all.
                                        —Isaac Watts

When the war in Korea first broke out, a woman fleeing from North Korea barely escaped with her life. When she was carried to a hospital, the doctor said, "Your feet will have to be amputated—it is the only way to save your life. Can you do without your feet?" He didn't know this woman was a Christian.

"I can do without my feet," she answered, "I can do without my hands. I can do without anything in this world, except Jesus!"

The Name of History

The person, nature, and name of Jesus Christ cannot be destroyed. We have had mighty people in this world, mighty men and women of war, mighty authors of literature, mighty artists and musicians, but none has had such impact on the world as Jesus Christ. By the spread of His Gospel, millions of lives have been transformed. His influence has operated through the centuries and the world is different from what it would have been without Him. Sin and evil permeated the course of mankind from the beginning, but salvation came only through Jesus Christ.

To some people, names are nothing more than a list in the telephone directory. But in the Bible we discover that the name of Jesus Christ implies the message God is trying to share with us. His Son's name, according to God's purpose, is to have preeminence. One historian has written that at the top of every page of history stands the name of Jesus, because Jesus walked across history. He has shaped our civilization.

Jesus changed the world's attitude toward childhood. In many non-Christian cultures, children have often been unwanted and were killed or abandoned. But in Christian lands, children are respected, valued, loved. There are laws in our nation against mistreating them. There are also homes for the children who have no one to care for them.

Jesus also changed the status of womanhood. In His time, women were often considered mere possessions, little more than slaves or animals. The equality and freedom women have in the enlightened parts of the world are the result of Christian principles applied in society.

He has changed the world's attitude toward the sick and afflicted. Once they were cast off from society, but the Great Physician taught us compassion and instituted ideals of healing.

William Wordsworth wrote, "Milton, thou shouldest have lived unto this hour!" Such a gifted man, had he lived on, might have continued to contribute to society, for he had made the world a better place in which to live. But as we call the roll of the mighty men of all ages, we have to remark concerning most of them, "It is better that the world forget such people as the Pharaoh of the Exodus and Genghis Khan and Adolf Hitler."

If you go to a rural cemetery and push back the weeds that overrun the markers, you will find names of those whose voices were powerful in the community of the past, who were able to control the lives and destinies of others while they lived. Now you can walk over their graves as easily as over those of the most helpless. All have been equalized with the passing of time—and death.

But Jesus has no grave over which the sacrilegious may tread with impunity—only an empty tomb into which we can gaze with awe. For Jesus lives until this hour. His name is the enduring name. Jesus Christ is still alive! He is alive forevermore!

Pilate, if he were living today, would still be trying to wash his hands, symbolically trying to remove from his soul the guilt, and from his mind and heart the memory of Jesus' name.

Judas, when he came to that dark garden at midnight, had beguiled himself into thinking that he was kissing the son of Mary, when He was touching the very face of God.

A French infidel named Voltaire once boasted, "One day I shall crush the wretch Jesus Christ." But when Voltaire lay dying, he cried out, "O Thou pale Galilean, Thou hast conquered!"

The Name of Hope

How could Jesus Christ be removed from this world? You would have to remove life, for He is Life. You would have to do away with truth, for He is Truth. You would have to forego healing, for He is the Great Physician. You would have to forget teaching for He is the Master Teacher. You would have to negate power, for He possesses all power. You would have to burn down churches, for He is the head of the church. You would have to destroy homes, for He is the heart of the home. You would have to blot out all hope, for He and He alone is the hope of the world.

The Gospel of hope flowered at the Cross. Only Jesus Christ could pay the penalty; only He could bear our sin. But the cross without the empty tomb was incomplete. The power of Jesus in our world today is the presence of a living Christ. Isaiah said His name was to be "Immanuel—God with us." This is more than a Christmas verse—it is a verse for the darkest night. It is a verse for "the valley of the shadow of death." It is a verse for the lonely hour, for the desolate heart. It is a verse for the stress and testing of temptation.

"Immanuel—God with us!" May we apologize to the Holy Spirit of God for our attitude when we live and act as if God were dead. We are so often tempted to think that God can't do anything with this evil world. But Jesus Christ is with us, and in Him is all power.

The Apostle Paul put a blunt question to those who were not living pure lives: "Know ye not that your body is the temple of the Holy Spirit?" (1 Cor. 3:16) This same Spirit is "Christ in you, the hope of glory" (Col. 1:27).

How better could we describe His presence with us? He is our only Saviour. He is our Confidant, our Counselor. He is our Friend, closer than a brother, who never leaves us or forsakes us. He knows all about us, "warts and all," and yet loves us supremely. He is our Great Physician, the only one who can give balm for our aching hearts, sleep to our weary bodies, rest to our troubled minds, cleansing to our sinful souls. He is indeed our hope of glory.

What greater name can we call Him than what God named Him: Jesus Christ, anointed Saviour and Deliverer? When we try to express in words what He has meant to us, it is difficult. But, bless God, we are able to say of His name, "It will do when I am dying!" This is the name, the only name, that you can whisper at the gate of heaven to find a loving welcome from the heavenly Father. For Jesus said, "Him that comes unto Me I will in no wise cast out" (John 6:37).

13 His All-Sufficient Priesthood

1 Timothy 2:5

Risen and ascended, our victorious Lord Jesus Christ is the continuing Christ.

It is paradoxical that though Jesus completed His work, it yet continues. The word *finished* can never be written over the work of Jesus. The Aramaic word He uttered on the cross is translated by three words in English: "It is finished" (John 19:30). In the Greek text, it is only one word, which does not mean "finished" in the sense that it left nothing more to be added, but that it was "fulfilled"—the crucial event prophesied had come to pass. Even now, Christ is tending to all that is necessary for the complete maturing of our salvation.

The earthly work of Jesus, from His birth and ministry to His death, resurrection, and ascension, was described by the Gospel writers plainly and in detail. But forty days after His resurrection, Jesus Christ ascended into heaven. He disappeared from His disciples' sight and the angels announced to them, "This same Jesus . . . shall so come in like manner" (Acts 1:11).

But, in between, what is happening in heaven and on earth?

Surely heaven is a perfect paradise we can't possibly imagine. And it is timeless—no past, present, or future as we understand them. But what is the relationship of Jesus Christ to His children on earth today? The Bible assures us that all Christians are joint heirs with Christ. From the time of His ascension into heaven, until He shall come back as victorious conqueror to the earth, He is our Redeemer and Intercessor. He passed beyond the curtain that separates heaven and earth into the divine holy of holies.

Satisfying God's Demands

One commentator has observed that to understand the Gospel, you must understand the Book of Romans, and to understand both the Law and the Gospel, you must understand the Book of Romans and the Book of Hebrews. The key word throughout Hebrews is *better*: the better priest, the better prophet, the better covenant. The writer of Hebrews masterfully sets forth a comparison of the Law and the Gospel, emphasizing the better things of grace in Jesus Christ. He is prophet, priest, and king, and "He ever lives to make intercession for them [His own]" (Heb. 7:25).

His redemptive work of sacrifice for sin was completed on Calvary. Every requirement for our salvation was satisfied. It was finished in every sense that men comprehend completion. But Jesus had a perspective about His work that none of us can know or understand.

We would welcome a chance to redo almost everything we have done, so we might do it better. Whatever song we sing, whatever message we give, whatever lesson we teach, whatever responsibility we fulfill—there so often comes the gnawing sense of incompleteness. If only we had that hour, that moment, to live over again! But Jesus accomplished His purpose completely; nothing was left to be perfected. "It is finished," He cried. His sacrificial death shattered all the foes of God and opened the gates of divine redemption. It perfected the mission that Jesus had come to accomplish.

It is a towering thought that He is the *remaining* Christ. We have many things that remain. The Bible remains. Jesus said, "Heaven and earth shall pass away, but My words shall not pass away" (Matt. 24:35). Jesus Christ is "the same yesterday, and today, and forever" (Heb. 13:8). The fact that He remains the continuing Christ is one of the thrilling miracles of all ages.

Hearing Our Pleas

Jesus Christ is now in the presence of God. What then is His relationship to us there, and what does it have to do with our lives here? First of all, we have in Him an advocate, a friend at court.

Many Old Testament characters seem to have longed for more closeness to God. Job expressed the desperate need that all men feel at one time or another: "Oh that I knew where I might find Him [God]" (Job 23:3). Job wanted to pour out the emptiness of his soul, the sin of his life, the love of his heart. He longed to have a closer walk with God. If only God could have been as real and near to Job as He was to Adam and Eve! At first, God had fellowship with the pair He created in the Garden of Eden. Then, because of sin, the face of God was veiled from men. Job was not the first man—or the last—to feel and express his need for God. All of us have a pressing need for God in our lives.

Certainly, God didn't have to enter earth to understand the hearts of men. But it was divinely necessary for Jesus to come here that *man might understand* the heart of God. His coming brought God nearer to us. We come to know God as He is revealed in the person and face of Jesus Christ.

"I go to prepare a place for you," Jesus promised His disciples (John 14:2). "But the Comforter . . . the Holy Spirit . . . the Father will send in My name, and He shall teach you all things" (John 14:26). He is the One who continues the work of Jesus on earth. The Holy Spirit "shall not speak of Himself, but . . . He shall glorify Me" (John 16:13-14). The Spirit always praises Jesus. Those who place so much emphasis on the Holy Spirit need to recognize that nowhere in the Scriptures does He put Himself forward, but rather magnifies the Godhead of which He is a part. He brings God closer to us and vice versa.

Jesus left this sin-cursed earth and returned to heaven, the Bible asserts, to sit down at the right hand of God. This indicates the nearness of Christ to His Father's heart. "The Lord said unto My Lord," wrote David, "Sit Thou at My right hand, until I make Thine enemies Thy footstool" (Ps. 110:1; cf. Mark 12:36). Part of the redemptive work of Jesus is to sit down beside the Father, having completed the sacrifice for our sins.

When Stephen was being stoned to death, the Bible records "He, being full of the Holy Ghost, looked up steadfastly into heaven, and saw the glory of God, and Jesus standing on the right hand of God" (Acts 7:55). Jesus was not sitting, but *standing*. The only time in the Bible we find God in a hurry is when He was pictured as the father running to welcome home his prodigal son (Luke 15:20). In the story of Stephen, we view the intense interest on the part of Jesus when one of His children is dying. No longer was Jesus sitting, but standing!

It is hard for us to comprehend God's tremendous interest in us. God has been drawn close to us and we are drawn close to Him by the intercession of Jesus. That is why, when we pray to God, we pray in Jesus' name.

Touching Our Tears

T. DeWitt Talmadge once made some pastoral calls with his wife, leaving their child with a babysitter. When they returned to the parsonage and opened the door, the child's back was toward them and he was playing quietly. But as soon as he saw his mother, he began to cry.

"What's wrong?" the mother asked.

"I hurt my hand."

"Why, I didn't see you hurt your hand," she said.

"I hurt my hand while you were away," the child insisted.

"Why didn't you cry then, instead of now?" the mother asked.

"Because I didn't have you to cry to," the child sobbed, running into his mother's arms.

There is a desolate feeling of loneliness in mankind, a frustration of longing that only God can satisfy. In Jesus, "we have not an high priest who cannot be touched with the feeling of our infirmities" (Heb. 4:15). Notice that it does not state He is touched *by* our infirmities, but He is touched *with* our infirmities.

Some take an attitude like those who passed by that injured man on the Jericho road. They looked down at him and were touched by the sight. "It is a terrible thing," they must have commented sadly, shaking their heads. "Someone ought to do something!"

Even though we are touched by the sins of the lost world, we often withdraw, not wanting to become involved. Jesus didn't withdraw. He plunged into the very midst of human life. He involved Himself in our feelings and our infirmities. Our suffering is not apart from Him; the suffering of His children is also His own suffering.

Many years ago I went to stay at the home of a rancher one night after a meeting. "Preacher," he confided in me out of a heart full of sorrow, "if your children are not yet old enough to break your heart, you have never known what real heartbreak is!" He was suffering with, not apart from, his children; there is such a close bond between a child and loving parents.

In the same kind of relationship, Jesus would have us understand that He feels with us the same intensity of joy or pain—and to a much greater degree. "If ye then, being evil, know how to give good gifts unto your children," He said, "how much more shall your heavenly Father give the Holy Spirit to them that ask Him?" (Luke 11:13)

He is touched *with* the feeling of our infirmities! We are prone to overlook and minimize the sufferings of others. You and I can know and understand only partially, but Jesus *knows* and understands *all* the sufferings of mankind. Others can understand your suffering only through comparison with whatever suffering they might have experienced. But not so with Jesus. There is no path to which we are called but that He has first gone before us to smooth it and blaze the trail.

One day a mother brought her desperately sick child into a hospital, and in the waiting room the child died. Neither the coaxing of the physician nor anyone else could make the woman give up her baby. Her husband came from his work, but not even he could persuade her.

A pastor was called and could do nothing. Finally, in the hospital corridor he saw a woman who had lost a child. "Will you sit down by her and talk to her awhile?" he asked. That mother who had gone through the same kind of bereavement poured out her heart of sympathy to the mother who was clutching her dead baby. After a few minutes of sharing their sorrow, touched by the other woman's heartfelt understanding, the grieving mother reached out and put the lifeless body into her hands. But it was only after someone had sat down by her side and suffered *with* her.

God does not offer us a spectator religion. He is not sitting in the balcony of heaven unmindful of our burdens and problems in this life. In Christ, God is immensely real and near. He understands the fine print of pain in our lives. He knows the silent heartaches we cannot share with anyone. Jesus is "touched with the feeling of our infirmities."

No one could say that Muhammad was touched *with* the sorrows of his people. The priests of false religions are not touched *with* the infirmities of their followers, but we can claim a great High Priest who suffers with us, who was tempted in all points as we are—yet without sin.

Therefore, we find fulfilled in our lives the promises of Jesus. "For He said," declared the writer to the Hebrews, "I will never leave thee, nor forsake thee" (Heb. 13:5).

He went back to heaven so the Holy Spirit might come to work for us and through us. There is suffering all over the world—not merely in one country, one town, one home. To the Holy Spirit of God, there is no question of time or miles. We can come to our omnipresent High Priest in heaven with prayers that span time and distance, for through the Holy Spirit, Jesus can reach every heart.

Understanding Our Weaknesses

Jesus is the perfect Priest. In the Old Testament, the priest was the man who mediated. He was a dedicated man who had to meet many special requirements for the priesthood. Even so, priests were only human and had many imperfections—just as the preachers in our pulpits today. But the priests performed a work of mediation; they offered the sacrifices, and then the high priest carried the blood into the holy of holies; he was the one who stood between God and man.

Jesus is called the Great High Priest (Heb. 4:14). He is above all the others. Melchizedek, the ancient priest of the Old Testament, is pointed out as the pattern of the priesthood of Christ, who did not qualify by lineage as Aaron and others who were descended from Levi. The Bible does not mention the parentage of Melchizedek, or his death. The Aaronic priesthood descended from one generation to another. The Bible calls Jesus our High Priest who *ever liveth* to make intercession for us.

What is Jesus Christ doing now? He is removing the stumbling blocks between us and God. The Bible teaches that as we pray, He takes our thoughts and our words and deciphers their true meaning. He understands and makes them as they ought to be: "Here is what My child is saying," He reports to the Father. He removes the obstacles of our ignorance and weakness. He remains there always to present our case at the throne of God.

The high priestly prayer of the Saviour is recorded

in John 17. "Those that Thou gavest Me I have kept," Jesus said to His Father (v. 12). He is always keeping us.

He is always speaking about us, always concerned about us. "I have prayed for thee," He assured Peter, "that thy faith fail not" (Luke 22:32). He is our praying Priest.

He is our personal Priest. Each of us has the right to come to the throne of God through Him. We can lay hold of the Father and boldly testify, "We have a Saviour and High Priest!" We have access to the throne of God, not because of anything good about us, but because of Him, our substitute.

Thus He is the perfect Advocate. He is not only the sacrificial Lamb, without spot or blemish. He is not only the Lifegiver through His shed blood, but He is the Mediator between God and man. Paul wrote to Timothy: "For there is one God, and one Mediator between God and men, the Man Christ Jesus" (1 Tim. 2:5).

When Jesus died that day on Golgotha, God reached down from heaven and ripped the veil of the temple from top to bottom. It would have taken the strength of about forty oxen to pull apart that heavily-woven linen curtain. Indeed, only the unseen hands of God could have torn it from top to bottom. No longer was God's mercy seat to be hidden; the avenue into His presence was opened for all eternity.

"Thou therefore, my son, be strong in the grace that is in Christ Jesus," Paul encouraged his protege, Timothy (2 Tim. 2:1). If you have Christ, then heaven is open to you. The ear of God, the presence of God, and the promises of God are available to you. We have, therefore, a *continuing* Christ, the Holy Son of God at the right hand of the Father, who ever lives to make intercession for us.

14 His Promised Indwelling

Romans 8:9

At present, Jesus Christ is not only with the Father, He is with us here. He promised His disciples to send another One like Himself: "I will pray [to] the Father, and He shall give you another Comforter, that He may abide with you forever.... I will not leave you comfortless" (John 14:16, 18).

Many teachers of our day define three major spiritual epochs of history: the age of prophecy in the Old Testament, featuring God the Father; the days of fulfillment in the Gospels, featuring God the Son; and the age of the Spirit, which is the church era. Since His descent at Pentecost, the Holy Spirit is still revealing Himself in unusual ways and in amazing power.

Jesus taught that the Holy Spirit is "the Spirit of truth, whom the world cannot receive, because it sees Him not, neither knows Him ... for He dwells with you, and shall be in you" (John 14:17).

Why do we know so little about the Holy Spirit? Why do we so frequently turn off any talk of His work? Is it because we have twisted impressions and certain prejudices? Some undignified activities and overexpressed emotions in the name of the Spirit have been offensive to some, and have caused them to reject the whole idea. Have we become fearful and lacking in evidence of the power of the Spirit of God? Or is it that we are such a secular people that we really don't want to understand spiritual things?

"But ye are not in the flesh," wrote the Apostle Paul to the early Christians, "but in the Spirit, if so be that the Spirit of God dwell in you. Now if any man have not the Spirit of Christ, he is none of His" (Rom. 8:9).

Who (not *what*) is the Holy Spirit? *He* (not *it*) is the member of the Godhead who is continually in the believer's midst.

What and who is the Trinity? The Trinity consists of three Persons, yet is One: God the Father, God the Son, and God the Holy Spirit. Any illustration I use would break down, but let me express it like this: I am a son to my mother; I am a husband to my wife; I am a father to my children. Each one of these roles has its distinct relationship and activity, yet I am still the same person.

Similarly, God is three Persons, yet One. Dr. B.H. Carroll, founder of Southwestern Baptist Seminary, used a definition of the Holy Spirit which I like best: he wrote that the Holy Spirit is "the other Jesus." Why is He "the other Jesus"? Because the Holy Spirit does not speak of Himself, but glorifies Christ. The Holy Spirit glorifies Jesus, and Jesus glorifies the Father. The Trinity functions in completeness, never division.

Our Invisible, Invincible Companion

When Jesus was with men on earth, He was visible. He was perishable, though His body was only briefly in the grave. But God is spirit and so too is the Holy Spirit who has come since Jesus ascended into heaven. The Holy Spirit is invisible.

He is also invincible, thank God! We live in a disturbed era and are increasingly conscious of the influence of Satan; his works are more openly in the media today than ever before. We have to be clear about whether the Holy Spirit is a mere influence or whether He is a Person: God with us and in us.

If He is a Person, He is a power. Because the Holy Spirit is constantly with us and invincible to all the problems of this earth, we do not have to feel that we are in danger.

There are at least five symbols of the Holy Spirit referred to in Scripture. Oil, especially the anointing oil of the Old Testament, was one symbol. Water was another; the priests had to wash thoroughly before putting on their holy garments to serve God. The dove from heaven which descended on Jesus at His baptism was a third. Wind, the symbol that Jesus used when He was talking with Nicodemus, was a fourth. Fire was a fifth; the fire fell at Pentecost and the presence of the Spirit came on the disciples with power. Notice that three times powerful forces in nature are used to illustrate the Spirit's strength.

In John 14 we read about the Holy Spirit as companion. "Even the Spirit of truth ... He dwells with you, and shall be in you. I will not leave you comfortless; I will come to you," Jesus assured His disciples (John 14:17-18). In the bodily absence of Jesus, the Holy Spirit serves as our Companion.

Jesus' disciples had watched Him perform miracles; they had been with Him all of their truly spiritual lives, and yet they were like little children. When a young person realizes for the first time that he has to live without the physical presence of father and mother, it is a shattering experience. He has never known life without them.

The disciples thought they had been through hard times already. "Lord, we know not whither Thou go, and how can we know the way?" Thomas asked (John 14:5). In other words, "How are we going to get along without You?"

"I will not leave you orphans," His reassurance has been paraphrased. "I will come [send Him, the Holy Spirit] to you."

Mary and Martha were deeply grieved that Christ had not arrived in Bethany in time to save their brother, Lazarus, from death—or so they thought. Martha said, "Lord, if Thou had been here, my brother had not died" (John 11:21). Jesus, in bodily form, had to choose whether to be with the sisters in their hour of sorrow or to be across the Jordan until the time He chose to call Lazarus forth from the grave.

But the power and presence of the Holy Spirit are never absent from any one of us. He may be sanctifying those who worship in the church service. He may be convicting those who are absent. He may be comforting those who are sick. He may be helping that one who is bedfast. The Holy Spirit is our divine and ever-present Companion.

Becoming Aware of His Presence

Consider the Emmaus road experience. The two disciples were not conscious that this Person who walked alongside them was the risen Saviour. They thought Jesus was dead. At mealtime, they saw His hands and heard His prayer, and then they realized who He was. "Did not our heart[s] burn within us, while He talked with us by the way?" they marveled (Luke 24:32). What a difference! The coldness of their grief had been turned to warmth by His presence.

We don't have to beg God to be with us, though we may have to ask Him to first straighten out our lives spiritually (because God is not going to give until we ask Him). We may have to ask God, "Make us aware of Your presence and make us sensitive to Your Spirit." But we don't have to ask God to *be* here, because He promised He would be with us always, and especially that He would be with those in His house on the Lord's Day. "Where two or three are gathered together in My name, there am I in the midst of them" (Matt. 18:20).

Our prayer needs to be, "O God, make us aware of Your presence; make us aware of Your power!" Another name for the Holy Spirit is *Paraclete,* which means "the-one-called-alongside to help us."

His presence is too seldom acknowledged. Once I was called on suddenly to preach a funeral in a small Texas town. The preacher who was supposed to hold the funeral did not arrive. It was a trying time for the family, and I didn't even know them. I went to the office of the funeral home and asked where the family was. I wanted to speak a word of comfort. The funeral director opened the door to the room where they were gathered. They were passing around a bottle.

"Preacher," one man remarked, "you will have to understand that we need some spirits for the road."

"May I say to you," I replied, "that what you really need is *The* Spirit for the road—not spirits? You need the Spirit of God to go with you in your emptiness and sorrow, in your frustration and helplessness. You need the Spirit of God, the presence of God!"

People often say, "Oh, I wish I had lived in Jesus' day! I wish I had been there like Peter. I wish I could have been alive when He was living on earth!"

I have news for you. Because we have the Holy

Spirit, we do not just have memories of the Master. He is alive now! He is risen: He abides in our hearts. He will fill our souls with His presence. We don't have to live with memories of 2,000 years ago, because the presence of the Prince of Peace can be in our hearts this very day. "I will come in to him, and will sup with him," guaranteed the risen Christ (Rev. 3:20).

Enjoying His Fellowship

Communion within a family is beautiful, and within the family of God, the communion of the Spirit of God is particularly beautiful. In a special sense, as God's children, we are God's family on earth. We refer to ourselves sometimes as "the kingdom of God," and this is right, but we are also "the family of God": the sons of God, brothers and sisters in the faith, and mutual partakers in the communion of the Holy Spirit.

Phillips Brooks, a Boston pastor and pulpit great of the past, once wrote, "The great benediction of the Christian church never grows old and is never monotonous." One of its familiar forms reads, "The grace of our Lord Jesus Christ, and the love of God, and the fellowship of the Holy Spirit, be with us all evermore." The communion of the Spirit of God is the most gracious comfort any thirsty, hungry, helpless heart can grasp when he comes to the house of God to worship.

I visited with a man who shared with me how much the church meant to him in a difficult time of loss. This gentleman, in his shaking years, said, "Preacher, how do people get along without the church and the Lord? I am having a hard enough time as it is, and I couldn't stand it if I couldn't pray. I couldn't make it through these lonely days if it were not for friends of the years and the church!"

The early church was a fellowship, not a building, and neither is the church merely a building now. It didn't make any difference whether believers met in a cathedral, or a catacomb, or a tent—they were a fellowship. They didn't have an organization to promote; the Holy Spirit did the promoting. They prayed and asked the Holy Spirit to empower people for the offices that were needed.

They didn't have an organized brotherhood; they simply promoted brotherhood among all men. That is the kind of brotherhood we need. We love one another, but we do not gather only to love one another, though our expression of love for one another is a meaningful experience. When my family gathers around our table, the food never seems to taste as good if there is an empty chair. In the same way, when God's people gather to have their souls fed in the house of God, if there is a single empty heart or a single empty pew, the service is not quite as good.

The Holy Spirit promotes the communion of His people; this is part of His work. Most of all, He prompts us to adore Christ. Historically, Pentecost followed Calvary—in the plan of God it could not precede it.

Accepting His Help and Correction

The Holy Spirit who indwells also commands. He has the same attributes as the Father and the Son, which include emotion, intellect, and will. But what are His special tasks? He searches our hearts. He guides our utterances. He convicts of sin and leads to repentance. He cautions that there are things we ought not do. And most of all, the Holy Spirit is our great Teacher. If you don't understand God's Word, you need only ask the Spirit of God to teach you. Just be sure you're in the Word to begin with!

The Holy Spirit helps the Christian in his infirmities. Sometimes we claim Romans 8:28 as our favorite verse, but look at all the infirmities mentioned in the following verses. None of them can separate us from the love of God. Why not? Because the Holy Spirit will not allow it. He will enable us to rise above the circumstances of life.

Unless we acknowledge and seek the Holy Spirit, we are not aware of Him in the church building or away from it. God is as much with each of us today as He was with Peter, James, and John. Now they live on "the other side" with God. In the person of the Holy Spirit, Jesus lives still on this side, in our hearts.

The presence of the Holy Spirit with us and in us is not accidental, nor incidental, but fundamental. There is no preacher under heaven or above the earth who can convict men of their sins with orations or with logic. The only One who can convict is the Spirit of God. He may do it through the words of a minister, the lyrics of a song, the exhortation of a prayer, the reading of Scripture, the presence of a person, or the knock on a door. But the Holy Spirit does the convicting.

The Holy Spirit also sanctifies us, for He throws the searchlight of God into the corners and crevices of our souls where we have hidden our sins. The Holy Spirit searches them out. The all-seeing eye of God makes us face ourselves. Sanctification is not always a comfortable process, but how comforting it will be when it is completed.

Receiving His Filling

The still, small voice of God speaks by the Holy Spirit. Do you want to be conscious of the Spirit of God in your life? If you want to know that God is alive in your heart, then ask Him to make Himself known through the indwellng Holy Spirit and to teach you more about Jesus.

"Be filled with the Spirit," commanded the Apostle Paul. This is the need, the possibility, and the privilege of every Christian.

Holy Spirit, breathe on me,
until my heart is clean;
Let sunshine fill its inmost part,
with not a cloud between.
Breathe on me, breathe on me, Holy Spirit,
breathe on me;
Take Thou my heart, cleanse ev'ry part,
Holy Spirit, breathe on me.

—Edwin Hatch

Other books by R. Earl Allen

Bible Paradoxes
Christian Comfort
Strength from Shadows
Silent Saturday
Sign of the Star
The Personal Jesus
Persons of the Passion
Bible Comparatives
Speaking in Parables
Divine Dividends
Funeral Source Book
Days to Remember: Sermons for Special Days
Good Morning, Lord. Devotions for Hospital Patients
Prayers That Changed History
The Hereafter, What Jesus Said about It
For Those Who Grieve
Jesus Loves Me
Seven Words of Christ
Good Morning, Lord. Devotions for Times of Sorrow